Children Beyond Labels

Children Beyond Labels is an accessible guide to understanding standardised assessment and managing high incidence additional learning needs in the primary school. It offers jargon-free insight into the results of formal assessments, which are often used within professional reports, and cuts to the core of how primary education professionals and parents can identify, understand and best meet children's needs.

Offering a range of practical and manageable strategies, the book provides clear explanations of commonly used labels which reflect three of the four areas described within the *SEND Code of Practice (2015)*: Cognition and Learning; Communication and Interaction; and Social, Emotional and Mental Health. These categories are illustrated by eighteen detailed case studies of children from the author's own case work, each with their unique profiles of strengths, weaknesses and traits that can sometimes transcend category boundaries. Examples of these traits include:

- Dyslexia
- Autism Spectrum Disorders
- Specific Language Impairment
- Attention Deficit Hyperactivity Disorder
- Developmental Co-ordination Disorder
- Anxiety.

This is an invaluable guide to the range of different types of additional learning or special needs of children who are likely to be found in mainstream primary schools. It will be of interest to primary teachers, trainee teachers, teaching assistants, SENCOs/inclusion managers, parents and anyone working to support the needs of young children.

Rhian Spence is a freelance education consultant who specialises in supporting children with additional needs. She became interested in barriers to learning after qualifying as a primary school teacher and went on to study for a Master's degree. Rhian has since worked as a SENCO, Inclusion Manager and peripatetic Specialist Teacher. She is interested in the use of assessment to establish children's learning profiles and tailor programmes of intervention.

CHILDREN BEYOND LABELS

Understanding Standardised Assessment and Managing Additional Learning Needs in Primary School

RHIAN SPENCE

Routledge
Taylor & Francis Group

LONDON AND NEW YORK

First published 2019
by Routledge
2 Park Square, Milton Park, Abingdon, Oxon OX14 4RN

and by Routledge
711 Third Avenue, New York, NY 10017

Routledge is an imprint of the Taylor & Francis Group, an informa business

© 2019 Rhian Spence

British Library Cataloguing-in-Publication Data
A catalogue record for this book is available from the British Library

Library of Congress Cataloging-in-Publication Data
A catalog record for this book has been applied for.

ISBN: 978-1-138-58077-0 (pbk)
ISBN: 978-0-429-50712-0 (ebk)

Typeset in Univers
by Apex CoVantage, LLC

This book is dedicated to my husband, Simon. His patience and constructively critical eye have been invaluable.

Contents

Acknowledgements

I would like to thank the following people:

Children, colleagues and parents from all the schools that have allowed and continue to allow me the privilege of working with them;

My friend and former colleague, Anne Mugglestone, whose professional motivation and opinion have spurred me on;

My son, **Rhys**, for his encouragement, belief and shared passion for educational opportunity, along with **Jess**, who has provided a welcome and interested sounding board; and

My parents, **Jean** and **David Rees**, for their life-long, enduring support and interest.

Glossary of Terms

Absolute average – mid average point

Access Arrangements – adjustments that can be made to support pupils in the classroom and during tests, including National Curriculum Tests, such as use of readers and extra time

Age equivalents scores – when raw scores achieved within standardised assessments are converted to a corresponding age rating

Age-related performance – expected levels of achievement, dependent on school year group and chronological age, regardless of cognitive ability and personal baselines

Attention Deficit Hyperactivity Disorder (ADHD) – a collection of behavioural symptoms including inattentiveness, hyperactivity and impulsiveness

Autism Spectrum Disorders (ASD) – difficulties associated with social interaction and communication which impact on relationships, yet children with this *diagnosis* range on a spectrum from the high-functioning and cognitively able to those with more severe and/or generalised learning difficulties

Bell Curve – graphic representation of the expected distribution and range of outcome scores achieved within assessments

Child and Adolescent Mental Health Services (CAMHS) – the services within the NHS that assess and treat young people with issues associated with emotional and behavioural wellbeing

Chronological age – actual age in years and months

Co-existing needs – when children experience multiple barriers to learning which transcend and overlap category boundaries

Cognition and Learning – a category of need within the *SEND Code of Practice* associated with variations in aptitudes for learning and acquisition of knowledge, skills and understanding

Communication and Interaction – a category of need within the *SEND Code of Practice*, associated with development of speech, understanding, and use of language

Criterion-referenced assessment – where performance is measured against defined criteria, such as the number of high-frequency words recognised, or letter sounds known

Decoding – using phonic knowledge to break down words when reading

Developmental Co-ordination Disorder (DCD)/Dyspraxia – a learning difficulty that primarily affects the skills associated with co-ordination and movement

Dyslexia – a learning difficulty that primarily affects the skills associated with accurate and fluent word reading and spelling

Education Health and Care Plans (EHCPs) – legal documents, identifying an individual's special educational needs, necessary provision and funding. Written following statutory assessment, overseen by local authorities, and subject to at least annual formal review. Held by fewer than two percent of the school population.

Encoding – using phonic knowledge to build words for spelling

English as an Additional Language (EAL) – when the main language used at home is not English

Expressive Language – ability to join words to form spoken sentences, using the correct vocabulary and grammar

Fine motor skills – use of the small muscles of the fingers, toes, wrists, lips and tongue, enabling small movements such as picking up small items and holding a spoon

General Language Impairment/Language Delay – weaknesses with all aspects of speech and language and language skills often in line with weak general cognitive ability

Generalised/ Global Learning Difficulties/Global Developmental Delay – children presenting with relatively flat cognitive assessment profiles and weak performance across the board, learning at a slower pace than the majority

Gross motor skills – use of the large muscles in the arms, legs, trunk or feet, enabling use of large movements, such as rolling over and sitting

Inclusion Development Programme (from 2008) – promoted suggestions for including pupils in mainstream classes with additional needs associated with Dyslexia, Speech, Language and Communication, Autism and Behaviour

Inclusive Classroom Strategies – where classroom teaching is modified (tasks, expectations, promotion of *self-help*, environmental tweaks, showing empathy and understanding) to enable curriculum access

Key Stage One – Years One and Two

Key Stage Two – Years Three to Six

Letters and Sounds – the title of the Phonics Programme introduced nationally in 2007 to be followed by whole classes from the age of five, with the intention of equipping children with the phonic knowledge and skills to enable reading fluency by the age of seven

Mechanical literacy skills – reading and spelling *accuracy* as opposed to, for example, reading comprehension and writing composition

Mechanical numeracy skills – *knowledge* of number facts, such as tables, as opposed to application of knowledge for solving number-based word problems, for example

Moderate Learning Difficulties (MLD) – as a general guide, cognitive assessment outcomes will be around centile two and children are usually educated within mainstream provision

National Curriculum Tests – external tests taken by all children in Years Two and Six

Percentile (centile) scores – gained when raw assessment scores are converted, according to chronological age, allowing comparisons of cognitive ability among children of the same or different ages. The *higher* the score *out of one hundred*, the higher the achievement; absolute average is 50.

Personal baseline – stage of learning an individual is at regardless of age-related expectations

Personalised and differentiated classroom teaching – see *Inclusive Classroom Strategies*

Phonics – a method for teaching reading and spelling accuracy by hearing, identifying and using different sounds that distinguish one English word from another

Quality First Teaching – when classroom teaching is differentiated and personalised to meet the needs of most pupils

Raw scores – total number of correct responses within assessments

Receptive Language – ability to understand what is said

Scaled scores where the *absolute average is 10* – gained when raw assessment scores are converted, according to chronological age, allowing comparisons of cognitive ability among children of the same or different ages

School SEN Support – when school provides *in-house* support to children without *EHCPs* which is *additional to and different from* that provided for the majority, such as a programme to address identified needs and hopefully accelerate progress

SEND Code of Practice: 0–25 Years (2015) – statutory guidance for organisations which work with and support children and young people who have special educational needs or disabilities

Sensory and/or Physical – a category of need within the *SEND Code of Practice* associated with hearing, vision or multisensory impairment or other physically disabling conditions

Severe/Profound and Multiple Learning Difficulties (SLD)/(PMLD) – children presenting with more complex needs than those with MLD and likely to attend specialist settings. Cognitive assessment outcomes will be well below centile two.

Social Communication – ability to use and understand non-verbal language such as facial expression

Social, Emotional and Mental Health – a category of need within the *SEND Code of Practice* which highlights that mental health needs may be demonstrated via various behaviours, from disruptive or disturbing to withdrawn or isolated

Specific Language Impairment (SLI)/Language Disorder – where one or more aspects of language development are weak in relation to others and/or to general cognitive ability

Specific Learning Difficulties (SpLD) – children presenting with spikey or alpine assessment profiles with marked strengths, often in verbal and/or non-verbal ability, alongside marked weaknesses (Dyslexia and/or Dyspraxia may have been diagnosed.)

Speech clarity – ability to speak clearly using correct speech sounds

Standard scores *where the* **absolute average is 100** – gained when raw assessment scores are converted, according to chronological age, allowing comparisons of cognitive ability among children of the same or different ages

Standardised Assessments (examples at Appendix I) – published assessment materials which have been tested rigorously on children within the targeted age group to establish range of expected outcomes allowing comparisons between abilities of children of given ages.

Statements – the predecessor of *Education Health and Care Plans (EHCPs)*

Target tracking-systems – process used by schools for the regular monitoring of progress made by *all* pupils

Verbal Dyspraxia – a condition where specific difficulties with co-ordination, motor planning and control can impact on movements required for speech

Introduction

Casework

Much of my work is casework, involving assessments of children causing concern to schools. Working across several schools, I have numerous children referred, presenting in various ways and with a range of needs.

Advice reports arise from all casework and often I *discover* children in different settings with common profiles. Knowing that there will be other similar children, attending primary schools nationwide, it occurred to me that sharing a selection of profiles with a wider audience could provide a useful source of reference to others working with children and parents/carers, clarifying jargon and demystifying labels. Based on extensive and current practice, the decision to collate a selection of cases – for sharing – is, therefore, an extended outcome arising from my original work.

When working with each of these children, my initial aims were to establish their unique profiles, identifying relative strengths as well as areas for development. Cases have been categorised broadly into three sections, according to primary need, and bearing in mind three of the four areas of need as described within the revised **SEND Code of Practice: 0–25 Years** (2015):

- **Cognition and Learning**
- **Communication and Interaction**
- **Social, Emotional and Mental Health**

The fourth area of need is **Sensory and/or Physical**. It is not included in this book, being a field covered by other practitioners with the relevant specialist knowledge and skills. *In reality, many children present with a range of co-existing needs which transcend the boundaries.* Personally, I find it most helpful to think in terms of a primary need alongside any secondary areas.

The following selection of real cases focuses on children within mainstream primary school settings and includes some with *Education Health and Care Plans (EHCPs)/Statements,* others who are supported via *School SEN Support* and others who are assisted by personalised and differentiated classroom teaching. *All names have been changed.*

Establishing children's profiles and categorising needs are perhaps the most straightforward aspects of casework; responding appropriately to these can be more challenging. There are *no magic wands or silver bullet solutions*, but in my experience, simple tweaks to classroom practice or lifestyle or particular programmes and activities can make all the difference, as can collaboration between home and school.

Each section adopts the same format: a brief introduction explaining the category and sub-categories of need, followed by illustrative case examples and concluding with activities and strategies that experience has shown to be effective. *It is important to emphasise, however, that the impact of any strategy or activity depends on the rigour with which it is implemented/ delivered. Remember, too, that all children are unique and there are no hard and fast rules or foolproof strategies; sometimes, it is a case of trial and error and maximising use of whatever works best for an individual child.*

Assessment

I use a range of standardised assessment tools to gain insight into children's relative learning strengths and needs. Such assessments provide a method of comparing the abilities of children of given ages. Performance is measured and standardised against a child's chronological age (actual age in years and months) so that outcomes are fair to younger children (those with Summer Birthdays) within any school year group. An explanation of the standardised assessments I use can be found at Appendix I.

Outcomes can be reported in a number of ways: as *percentile scores*, out of 100, where the *absolute average (mid average point) for age is 50*; as *standard scores*, where the *absolute average for age is 100*; and, less frequently, as *scaled scores*, where the *absolute average is 10*.

Personally, I use percentile scores, alongside age equivalents. Whilst age equivalent scores are easy to understand, in my experience understanding of percentile scores is inconsistent. When my interest in assessment began I found use of standard scores and percentiles confusing. I remember being asked by a more experienced colleague whether I *thought* in terms of standard scores or percentiles; at the time, I was not at all sure!

With percentiles, essentially, the higher the score out of one hundred, the higher the achievement.

Percentile Descriptions

Percentile	Equivalent percentage of group of 100 children	Meaning
98 and above	2%	Well above average
84–97	14%	Above average
50–83	34%	High average
16–49	34%	Low average
2–15	14%	Below average
Below 2	2%	Well below average

In other words, for every hundred children of a given age, two would gain outcomes well below average, fourteen would gain outcomes below average, thirty four would gain low average outcomes with another thirty four gaining high average outcomes, fourteen gaining above average scores and two achieving well above average scores.

A **Bell Curve** representation of the detail in the table above can be useful for understanding. See Figure I.1 below.

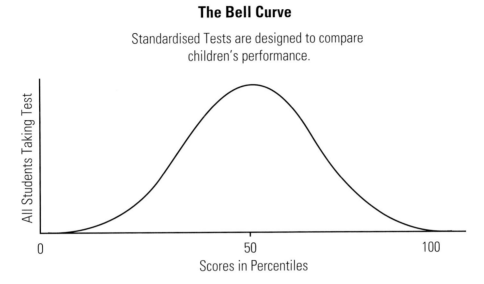

The Bell Curve

Standardised Tests are designed to compare children's performance.

Figure I.1 Percentile Percentages Bell Curve

The following are illustrative examples of explaining and interpreting percentile (centile) outcomes:

- Achievement at centile 77 equates to a score equal to or better than 77% of children of the same age (77/100). 23% would have achieved higher scores.
- Achievement at centile 2 equates to a score equal to or better than 2% of people of the same age (2/100). 98% would have achieved higher scores.

In addition to using standardised assessments, I make use of informal assessment when making judgements about performance. I observe children's approaches to tasks during one-to-one work and sometimes observe in other settings – the classroom and/or the playground. Generally, the younger the child, the more class-based observation is required. This allows for observation of social skills and general engagement, both prerequisites for success.

Often, my approach includes simple criterion-referenced assessment, where performance is measured against defined criteria, such as the number of high-frequency words recognised, or known phonics and ability to apply this knowledge for accurate decoding (reading) and encoding (spelling) of the printed word.

High frequency word and phonic checklists used can be found at Appendix II. These are from *Letters and Sounds*, the Phonics Programme introduced nationally in 2007 to be followed by whole classes from the age of five, with the intention of equipping children with the phonic knowledge and skills to enable them to become fluent readers by the age of seven.

Labels

Seeing children, beyond labels, is of paramount importance.

Experience suggests a focus and emphasis on *overcoming barriers* is more likely to enhance progress than *labels.* That said, labels can be useful in understanding difference and identifying the most appropriate strategies. Conversely, they can be negative, particularly when doggedly pursued and used too readily and/or too liberally. Sometimes, children are given multiple labels and acquisition of these can be something of a lottery. Some parents/carers actively seek labels as explanations for learning difficulties or slower than expected progress. Others resist them with passion and, of course, some labels can seem more acceptable than others in terms of perceived stigma. A danger is that the use of labels can provide excuses for low achievement or lack of progress – 'I/He/She can't do that because . . .!' These thoughts, and the danger that they will become self-fulfilling, can contribute towards mind-sets that need to be avoided.

When English as an Additional Language (EAL) masks additional/special learning needs

The increasing number of children with EAL in our schools is adding to the challenge of establishing and untangling potential additional/special needs. To what extent is slow or minimal progress due to having EAL or is EAL masking other needs? Increasingly, some children with EAL are presenting as more and more complex, sometimes with medical diagnoses. *Perhaps, this is because of growing awareness of our emphasis on a personalised and differentiated curriculum as opposed to a 'one size fits all' approach.* Some years ago, I came across a young boy of eleven with significant apparent barriers to learning, beyond EAL. He had been referred to me in the hope that I could begin to untangle his needs. He was quite frank, in the way children are, when asked why he had moved to England, 'My Mum . . . she bring me to England because she love me so much and here school easy. In my country, school *very* hard!'

Varying cultural priorities in approaches to teaching and learning

A further observation highlights other challenges some children face when leaving the education systems within their home countries to join ours. Approaches to teaching and learning and curriculum emphases are often poles apart, with hugely variable priorities *even when children have been taught through the medium of English.* On arrival in our schools, such children often present with good mechanical literacy skills: beautiful cursive handwriting, good spelling and reading accuracy. Alongside this, text reading comprehension, writing structure and content, understanding and use of language are often significant areas of weakness, according to our expectations.

Sometimes, such different educational priorities and experiences manifest themselves in the progress and performance of other children from ethnic minorities *even when they have been educated entirely within our system.* If their parents/carers were educated via a curriculum with different priorities, they (the parents) will often tend to emphasise the importance of mechanical literacy and numeracy skills above others, providing further opportunities to practise these skills at home; this can widen the gap between mechanical and other skills, rather than enhance all-round progress. My observations suggest that this is frequently the case where parents/carers are keen and aspirational but have limited understanding of the scope of our curriculum.

Emphasis on high quality class-teaching

At the core of the Code of Practice is emphasis on high quality class-teaching (*Quality First Teaching*) that is differentiated and personalised to meet the needs of most pupils. This promotes a cultural shift whereby all teachers are expected to be teachers of children with additional learning needs. In practice, as ever, some teachers will be more effective than others and some will be particularly effective with certain groups; we all have strengths and weaknesses, teachers included. Some children will respond favourably to certain teachers and styles of teaching and less so to others; what may seem a major issue and concern one year may disappear the next. We all respond to individuals differently; this is the way of the world.

There are so many inclusive classroom strategies that can enhance children's experience of teaching and learning and many of these are simple and easy to implement. It is true that often what works for one child, with particular needs, works for many others in a class too and, within some settings, modifications might be of benefit to the majority. It is also true that what is effective for one/some can be a significant hindrance to another/others. An 'all singing, all dancing' classroom, with extensive auditory and/or visual stimuli, will prove stimulating for many, but over stimulating and quite overwhelming to others.

Inclusive classroom strategies

Strategies for inclusion were promoted by the *Inclusion Development Programme* from 2008 and focused on including pupils with dyslexia, speech, language and communication difficulties, autism and behaviour needs in mainstream classes. These materials can now be acccessed as part of the *SEND Gateway*. This is a good resource but may seem overwhelming in terms of its scope. Accordingly, I have concluded each category of need section with succinct lists, as *aides memoire*, of what I consider to be some of the most useful and user-friendly inclusive strategies. They are by no means exhaustive lists but can help to make inclusion feel more manageable.

Consistent implementation of supportive strategies will help their use become incidental and automatic. Most of the strategies will not be *new* to experienced teachers, who will be implementing many already; hence my suggestion that they are viewed as an *aide memoire*.

Additional and/or different provision

Sometimes parents/carers (and some teachers) think of SEN provision solely as something *additional to and different from* that provided for the majority, a one- to-one programme, for example. We need to be educating beyond this expectation. This will be *sold* easily to some parents/carers, who dislike the practice of withdrawal from class and its potential for making children feel *different*; others will take more convincing.

Beyond the use of inclusive strategies, the Code of Practice, like its predecessor, recognises that some children will need provision that is additional to and different from this, either via *School SEN Support* or, when needs are more complex/severe, via an *EHCP/Statement*. Such support will focus on activities and programmes to promote skill development in addition to use of inclusive classroom strategies.

Explaining *Quality First Teaching* to parents/carers

It is probably worth clarifying with parents/carers what *Quality First Teaching* means: differentiation and personalised learning, whereby the curriculum is modified to become accessible to all children, through the incorporation of a range of strategies to ensure all are included, and tasks are pitched at appropriate levels. The ultimate aim of ensuring that all children can access lessons and learn at their own levels needs to be made crystal clear.

M.A.T.C.H. (Canchild) can be useful when explaining strategies and approaches employed by class teachers to parents/carers:

M Modify the task

A Alter your expectations

T Teach strategies

C Change the environment

H Help by understanding

Identifying strategies in use to keep parents/carers informed

The lists of strategies within each of Sections One, Two and Three of this book can also be useful for home-school liaison, clarifying and emphasising classroom strategies in place to support children's progress and learning. Some of my schools have provided parents/carers with highlighted copies, personalised according to provision made for their children.

Making parents/carers very aware of provision made within the classroom is essential as without doing this very clearly and directly there will always be those who claim the school is doing/ has done nothing. Many parents/carers are unaware, sometimes through no fault of their own, of differentiated, personalised provision made for their children within the classroom; it can be frustrating and disappointing when claims are made that nothing has been done, so transparency and clarity are a priority.

Home school partnership in the education process

No parent/carer or school is perfect, but collaboration between home and school is likely to lead to better outcomes, *whether or not children have additional/special needs*. Developing effective home-school partnerships where children do have additional/special needs is critical. Both parties will hopefully always have the child's best interests at heart, sharing common goals which are more likely to be achieved through joint effort and support.

Many parents/carers welcome working in partnerships with schools; others are less forthcoming, sometimes because they lack confidence, fear judgement or have negative memories of their own school experience. Most schools welcome working in partnership with parents and carers, realising its positive potential. Occasionally, schools can become less enthusiastic, particularly where demands made are unrealistic or involvement becomes obstructive and negative; in these circumstances the focus changes to schools doing their best in the absence of the parent/carer's active cooperation.

Parents/carers know their children best, often becoming their *Champions*, navigating the optimum routes to development through childhood, school and beyond. Parents/carers have less insight, however, into their children's contextual presentation at school. Viewing your own child objectively can be challenging, especially in the face of perceived criticism, stirring defensive feelings even within the mild mannered.

Successful partnerships require mutual respect and understanding, with schools promoting the view that *input from parents/carers is a positive asset. Accepting mutual imperfections and managing expectations* so that they are realistic, yet adequately aspirational, are necessary foundations for success.

Measuring and reporting on progress

The rigorous progress and target-tracking systems now in place in schools have led to greater clarity in reporting to all parents. In general, this is positive and can also contribute towards improved accountability.

It is pleasing to be told that your child's performance and progress meet or even exceed age-related expectations. On the other hand, it leads to inevitable disappointment to learn your child's performance falls below age-related expectations and compares unfavourably with that of peers. School contexts can exaggerate or understate apparent additional or different needs. For example, within a high achieving school, which is perhaps topping local authority league tables, children with low average ability and performance can seem to be experiencing relative learning difficulties. Within a more average school, ability and performance at the same levels are likely to be more the norm. That said, those with significant and complex needs will be very obvious, regardless of setting.

Some children face considerable barriers to learning, making age-related achievement impossible and, at times, it can feel like the system is setting them up to fail. Measuring performance in *smaller steps and from personal baselines* seems much fairer, more positive and, above all, encouraging. Everyone needs success at their own level: *success breeds success*. Beyond a sense of disappointment, continual failure can prove very demotivating.

Sometimes, parents of children with complex and multiple needs talk of their children *catching-up*. By this, they mean the time when performance and achievement at school is on a par with age-related expectations and peers, the gap minimised, eradicated even, as a result of additional provision by way of programmes and strategies. In these circumstances, parents/carers are sometimes described as being *in denial*. Sensitivity from schools is required to support their gradual acceptance that, while their child might never catch up, they can make progress.

Section 1
Cognition and Learning

Children present at school with varying aptitudes for learning and acquisition of knowledge, skills and understanding; both genetic and environmental factors influence these. They will usually demonstrate inherited patterns of learning strengths and weaknesses. Sometimes, other issues with development, from conception to birth and beyond, will override this.

Environmental influences can enhance or hinder progress or fall somewhere in between these two extremes. Levels of parental/carer interest, expectations, and capacity for providing incidental and enrichment learning opportunities can reduce or increase educational advantage. The environmental ethos within schools is also influential. Whilst a supportive environment provides children of all abilities with significant advantages, the degree of impact will, of course, depend on their levels of cognitive functioning.

Children with special/additional Cognition and Learning needs fall into two groups: those with *Specific*, and those with *Generalised* or *Global Learning Difficulties/Delay*.

Specific Learning Difficulties (SpLD) – insight

Sometimes parents seek the following labels as explanations of slow or slower than hoped for progress, even when school attainment is well within the average range. Such labels are often more acceptable to parents/carers than others. Perhaps they offer more hope and less stigma than labels associated with Generalised/Global Learning Difficulties, for example.

Children typically display some or all of the following signs:

- Low self-esteem/confidence/motivation
- Inconsistent performance with good days and bad
- Avoiding starting and/or rarely completing tasks
- Struggling to record (often good) ideas on paper
- Fatigue because of the extra effort required.

Dyslexia

The Rose Report (2009: 10) defines Dyslexia:

> *Dyslexia is a learning difficulty that primarily affects the skills involved in accurate and fluent word reading and spelling.*

Dyslexia is an educational issue, not a medical diagnosis, and is often hereditary. Assessment profiles tend to be spikey with particular strengths, often in verbal and/or non-verbal ability, alongside marked weakness with reading and /or spelling accuracy.

Developmental Co-ordination Disorder (DCD)/Dyspraxia

Unlike Dyslexia, DCD requires a medical diagnosis but is not caused by a general medical condition such as cerebral palsy or muscular dystrophy.

It is characterised by specific difficulties with co-ordination, motor (movement) planning and control which can affect any or all movements, including those required for speech (Verbal Dyspraxia). Fine and/or gross motor skills can be affected. Fine motor skills involve use of the small muscles of the fingers, toes, wrists, lips and tongue, enabling small movements such as picking up small items and holding a spoon. Gross motor skills describe bigger movements, such as rolling over and sitting; these rely on the use of large muscles in the arms, legs, trunk or feet.

Such impairments in movement planning and in the development of motor co-ordination interfere with academic achievement and the activities of daily living.

Children with DCD are likely to have been late in reaching motor milestones.

There may be issues with handwriting (legibility and/or speed), drawing, copying tasks, visual tracking (required for reading lines of print), organisation, attention, dressing and undressing, eating tidily, deciding which hand to use, hopping, skipping, throwing and riding a bike. As with Dyslexia, assessment profiles of children with this diagnosis tend to be spikey with notable areas of strength.

It is not unusual for children to present with traits of both Dyslexia and DCD/Dyspraxia. It can be useful to think in terms of spectrums, with some experiencing mild traits, through to others facing persistent and substantial barriers.

Specific Learning Difficulties case examples
(Evie, Owen, Matthew and David)

Evie

Evie presented with Dyslexia traits, identified at an early stage. We first met when she was four years, nine months and in a Reception class. We met again, for monitoring purposes, when she was in Year One and for a third time when she was in Year Two.

When Evie and I met for the *first* time, Reception Class Teacher had observed significant difficulties with the retention of phonics for reading. Class Teaching Assistant had noted inability to apply phonics for reading words and non-words, *even when sounds were given.*

Observation in class demonstrated good turn-taking and ability to follow collective instructions, effective cutting and sticking, ability to focus and work independently on self-selected, practical tasks. When older children arrived to facilitate book sharing with *buddies,* Evie showed minimal interest, causing her assigned buddy to give up. When reading with Teaching Assistant on a one-to- one basis, Evie recognized several high frequency words *by sight.* She required encouragement, yet tried hard, to decode other words. Evie recognized her limited success, commenting, 'I don't know many!'

During a whole class activity (high-frequency word/picture matching), where children were encouraged to *sound words out in heads* to support decoding, before raising hands to volunteer answers, Evie was often disengaged, fiddling with her fingers and head bowed. She volunteered occasional responses, decoding *bus* as *bed,* but reading *fox* correctly (her class group's name and probably recognised by sight).

One-to-one work with Evie highlighted good understanding of vocabulary (demonstrated below by scored outcome with the ***British Picture Vocabulary Scale***). Her outcome score, at age equivalent five years, seven months and percentile eighty-three, fell at the very top end of the high average range for her chronological age.

Chronological Age:	4.09	Test Age	Centile
British Picture Vocabulary Scale – 3rd Edition	5.07	83	

Evie shared with me that she liked school, but disliked reading and admitted to not practising at home – 'I say *no* to Mummy!' She identified her favourite toy as 'a beautiful *snuggly* unicorn', demonstrating her effective use of expressive (spoken) language.

Evie knew she would be five in April and wrote her first name accurately, although entirely in capital letters. A left-hander, she applied a suitable pencil grip.

Informal assessment of *ability to discriminate between sounds, without viewing lip actions*, suggested some weakness, with Evie repeating let/net as net/net, pit/bit as bit/bit, pot/top as hot/top, shut/just as shut/dust, raw/war as war/war and in/on as on/in. Weakness with *sound blending, again without viewing lip actions*, was also evident. Evie was unable to blend the sounds provided to build the following words and non-words: c-a-t (said add), f-a-t (said fed), l-e-t (said lid), p-o-t (said hot), p-e-g (said beg), f-eet (said eat), d-u-p (said p . . .), p-o-g (said pomp). She was successful with l-i-p, b-oa-t and sh-o-p.

My initial conclusions were that Evie's profile (good vocabulary and general ability, alongside weaknesses with acquisition and application of phonics for word-building) suggested a *Specific Learning Difficulty* (*Dyslexia*). At this early stage, however, it was not possible to forecast the degree of difficulties that Evie would experience in future. It was to the credit of Class Teacher and Teaching Assistant that her particular issues with phonics were identified at such an early stage in her school career. Early identification enabled the implementation of appropriate approaches sooner rather than later.

Evie and I met for the second time when she was five years, five months.

When we met again, eight months later, for monitoring purposes, Evie had transferred to Year One. Update assessment outcomes (see below) confirmed appropriate progress with vocabulary (**British Picture Vocabulary Scale**), alongside an age appropriate score for her drawing of a person (**Goodenough Draw-a-Person**).

Chronological Age:	5.05		Test Age	Centile
British Picture Vocabulary Scale – 3rd Edition			6.02 (+7 months over 8 months)	78
Goodenough Draw a Person Test (Aston Index)			5.09 (Not used before)	–

Evie's transition from Reception seemed to have been smooth. She identified *writing*, as a personal strength, and mentioned her enjoyment of reading. Socially, too, she seemed well integrated with many friends and interests, both in and beyond school. With adults, Evie engaged well, making good eye contact, maintaining topics of conversation and co-operating with all tasks presented.

Although ability to discriminate between and blend sounds for word-building had improved, Evie had no success with blending sounds to make non-words: dup (dob), pog (dog), gapo (gep) etc.

By this stage, Evie recognised all initial letter sounds, apart from *q* and was able to use this knowledge to read 10/25 *consonant vowel consonant* words (e.g. cot, sit). Most errors involved *b/d* confusion or inaccuracies with final letter sounds. Evie could, by now, read most **Phase 2** high-frequency words (26/32), recognising some by sight and applying phonics to decode others.

Evie was now competent at writing her full name, still using her left hand and applying an efficient pencil grip. She also understood the concept of a simple sentence and was able to verbalise one about herself, 'I like flowers.' Evie was reluctant to have a go at writing this when unsure of spelling, 'I have no idea how to write *like*!' Watching my lips, as I said *like* helped her to identify the initial letter correctly. Despite this, she showed awareness of word boundaries, using her finger to space written words. Beyond confusion between *b* and *d*, Evie was able to write letters to match all single sounds, producing generally well-formed letters, with clear *ascenders* (as in *h*, *t*) and *descenders* (as in *g*, y,). She managed the correct spelling of only 1/10 *consonant vowel consonant* words, usually producing the correct initial sound, but confusing the medial vowel and/or final letter sound.

Evie and I met for the third time when she was six years, six months.

When we met again, ten months later, for continued monitoring purposes, Evie had transferred to Year Two. At that time, Class Teacher assessed performance in reading and writing as just below average, according to national expectations; she also commented on Evie's excellent leadership skills. Again, Evie highlighted *writing* as an area of personal strength, and also character traits of which she was proud, 'Being nice to people and being friendly.' She mentioned her continued enjoyment of school, despite some reservations since progressing to Year Two, 'It's a lot of hard work! We have to do tall letters and small letters!'

Evie remained unsure about the letter *q*, again giving the letter name rather than its sound. This time, she was able to make use of sounds for accurate reading of 24/25 *consonant vowel consonant* words, as opposed to 10/25 previously, and also demonstrated ability to apply phonics for decoding non-words. Evie demonstrated retention of a number of **Phase 3** graphemes (e.g. sh, ch), but sometimes reverted to giving single letter names when unsure. She had to think *really* hard to use and apply this knowledge for reading words, but achieved some success.

On this occasion, Evie was able to read forty-one additional words from across **Phases 2–5**, often applying phonics with rigour, although she recognised many words by sight. At times, she confused visually similar words. When reading a short passage, Evie made no use of pictures or context to support reading accuracy, but she was able to answer a series of closed questions demonstrating accurate comprehension.

When writing, Evie seemed to have largely overcome her *b/d* confusion, but was uncertain of the orientation of the letter *j*. Today, she was able to write 10/10 *consonant vowel consonant* words accurately, as opposed to just one previously. Evie was also able to use a few graphemes for accurate spelling (ship, chop and cow). *Thin* was written as *fin*. She was also able to spell most **Phase 2** and some **Phase 3** words.

Evie readily verbalised an interesting sentence about her holiday, before having a go at writing it, 'I went to Majorca because it was my Mum's Birthday.' When requested, she verbalised a second sentence before writing it, 'We went on a boring trip around the Island.'

Evie did not use her free, non-writing hand to stabilise the paper and handwriting deteriorated as a result, becoming large and unwieldy. She started both sentences well, before seeming to lose track of words written mid-sentence. Evie made some use of correct spelling in context and use of accurate phonics where she was unsure. When writing the word *on* Evie wrote *n* first before squeezing in the letter *o* in front. Evie was much more prepared to have a go with spelling, when unsure, than previously.

Despite measurable progress with mechanical reading and spelling skills, the level of effort required from Evie was observed to be considerable, demanding a great deal of persistence. *When Evie reached the end of Year Two, although parents recognised progress made, they decided to leave the state sector, opting for mainstream, private education, with smaller classes, which they hoped might be beneficial.*

Owen

Owen presented with traits of Dyslexia and DCD/Dyspraxia, although he had no formal diagnosis of the latter. His specific learning difficulties may have been compounded by a busy, bordering chaotic lifestyle, with some of his behaviours suggesting anxiety and fatigue. We met when he was six years, six months and in Year Two. His assessment profile (see below) was very uneven: robust general cognitive ability (demonstrated by scored outcomes with the *British Picture Vocabulary Scale, Digit Repetition Test of Short-term Auditory Memory, Raven's*

Coloured Progressive Matrices test of non-verbal ability and *Goodenough's Draw-a-person test*) alongside specific difficulties with reading and writing skills (including weak standardised scores in reading and spelling).

Chronological Age:	6.06	Test Age	Centile
British Picture Vocabulary Scale – 3rd Edition (Understanding Vocabulary)		7.11	70
Short Term Auditory Memory: Digit Repetition		–	40
Raven's Coloured Progressive Matrices (Aspects of non-verbal ability)		–	37
Goodenough Draw-a-Person		6.09	–
Single Word Reading Test (nfer Form 2)		5.06	16
Vernon Spelling Test – 3rd Edition		–	2
Text Reading: Neale Analysis of Reading Ability (Form 2)	Accuracy	< 6.01	20
	Comprehension	< 6.01	< 2

Owen had been referred to me because of Class Teacher's concerns regarding markedly slow progress with reading, spelling and writing skills, despite an extensive vocabulary and particularly good ideas in Science. Class Teacher described Owen's considerable limitations with ability to record in writing and commented on his permanently fatigued presentation at school.

Discussion with Owen confirmed that he did not much enjoy school, commenting, 'It's *really* long!' Further discussion highlighted that he enjoyed Tuesdays and Fridays most because of the activities on offer. On Tuesdays, he enjoyed the range of activities at school: cooking, drama and making puppets. On Fridays he had swimming lessons after school, 'I don't know how to swim much yet. My Dad's put my goggles *mega* tight!'

Day-to-day Owen liked lunchtimes most, 'I have hot dinners and don't know what I'm going to get. My Mum and Dad give me *humungus* packed lunches sometimes!' When asked what he was *good at doing*, Owen commented, '*I'm not very good* at loads of stuff.' When asked what he finds hardest, at school, Owen was quick to respond, 'Oh man! *Guided reading* time and all other lessons!'

Owen considered that he had lots of friends and mentioned one in particular, 'He lives at my house with his family. Their house is broken. A tree fell on the house. A construction worker can't fix this much damage!' Owen also mentioned sharing his bedroom and bunk bed with his friend.

When not at school he was clear about his preferred activities, 'I play X-Box and *hang out* all day long. I am the boss of my family!' He indicated his dislike of homework as he would prefer to play on his X-Box. He also talked of living at his Mum's house and his Dad's house, explaining, 'They are separated. When I'm a teenager I can go to any house I want.'

Owen spoke very quickly which impacted on intelligibility. He tended to go off at tangents in conversation, flitting from topic to topic, telling me about his Auntie's dog one minute and his favourite footballer the next. Owen gave some eye contact although maintenance of this was erratic. Throughout the time we worked together, he made continual sounds, fidgeted somewhat and often grimaced, apparently involuntarily.

When drawing, Owen used his right hand, making use of his left hand to stabilise paper. He employed a somewhat awkward, four fingered pencil grip (thumb and three fingers resting on the pencil). The pencil sloped away from, rather than towards him and did not, therefore, rest on the web between thumb and index finger.

When writing, Owen's face was positioned very near the page and use of his left hand to stabilise paper was inconsistent. He was able to verbalise a sentence about himself, 'I like staying at home because I like playing with my toys.' As he attempted to write this sentence, Owen sought to employ phonic strategies to aid spelling, whispering the sounds within words to himself. He produced a shortened version of the sentence with some correct spelling in context – 'I like staying at home.'

Owen wrote a simple sentence accurately, from dictation – *It is not hot.* In terms of handwriting, there were a number of issues: inadequate spaces between words, random use of capital letters mid-word/sentence, poor letter formation, including insecurity with orientation of some, and erratic positioning of letters on lines.

Beyond his very weak standardised spelling test score, at centile two, Owen was able to spell 23/32 high frequency words from **Phase 2** and 7/10 *consonant vowel consonant* words accurately. He wrote his first name correctly and, with encouragement, had a go at writing his surname.

When reading, Owen applied phonic strategies accurately to decode single words, such as *yes, big, went, for, toy, back, chin* and *cry*. He also used phonics when text reading, but needed to do so, word-by-word, so that it became a laborious exercise, allowing little scope to read for meaning. Standardised scores for reading accuracy fell just within the low average range for chronological age at centiles sixteen and twenty. His score for reading comprehension, at below centile two, was very weak because of limitations with reading fluency and the effort required to decode print, rather than issues with understanding the language involved. Interestingly, Owen mentioned wearing glasses for reading, 'I only wear glasses for reading at Dad's house. I don't need them at school.'

Matthew

Matthew presented with diagnosed DCD/Dyspraxia. Occupational therapy assessment highlighted particular weaknesses with balance and manual dexterity. We met when he was nine years, eight months and in Year Five. Matthew's standardised assessment profile (see below) indicated robust general cognitive ability (demonstrated by scored outcomes with the *British Picture Vocabulary Scale, Digit Repetition Test of Short-term Auditory Memory, Raven's Coloured Progressive Matrices test* of non-verbal ability and *Goodenough's Draw-a-person test*). Matthew's attainment scores in spelling and reading were also strong, but ability to record in writing was hampered by his DCD/Dyspraxia.

Chronological Age:	9:08	Test Age	Centile
British Picture Vocabulary Scale – 3rd Edition (Understanding Vocabulary)		11.0	66
Short Term Auditory Memory: Digit Repetition		–	77
Raven's Coloured Progressive Matrices (Aspects of non-verbal ability)		–	91
Goodenough Draw-a-Person		9.06	–
Single Word Reading Test (nfer Form 1)		11.06	77
Vernon Spelling Test – 3rd Edition		9.10	54
Text Reading:	**Accuracy**	12.02	86
Neale Analysis of Reading Ability (Form 2)	**Comprehension**	12.08 +	80

Matthew was referred to me at the request of his Occupational Therapist who sought insight into his cognitive ability. Class Teacher commented on his slow writing speed and the discrepancy between this and ability to engage well in discussions. She had also observed his tendency to work from right to left and from the bottom of the page up.

Discussion with Matthew confirmed his limited enthusiasm for school. He considered *maths* a personal strength and shared no concerns regarding writing.

Initially, Matthew presented as somewhat nervous, but he sat still, remained focused and co-operated with all tasks. Although rarely initiating or extending conversation he responded appropriately, becoming quite animated when telling me about his pets and supporting Tottenham Hotspur Football Club.

When drawing, Matthew applied a right-handed pencil grip and made use of his left hand to stabilise paper, but sometimes moved the paper around, keeping the pencil still, rather than moving the pencil over the page. When writing, unlike when drawing, Matthew's non-writing hand often became a *headrest*, with his head positioned very close to the page.

Matthew engaged in a *ten minute write* about someone he knows well; he chose to write about his Mum. He managed just three sentences, but all made sense with correct punctuation and spelling in context. Handwriting was legible, with letters well positioned on lines and adequate spaces left between words. Letter size was inconsistent, as was beginning new lines next to the margin.

David

David presented with traits of DCD/Dyspraxia but had no formal diagnosis. We met when he was eight years, eleven months and in Year Four. David's standardised assessment profile (see below) indicated robust general cognitive ability (demonstrated by scored outcomes with the *British Picture Vocabulary Scale, Digit Repetition Test of Short-term Auditory Memory* and *Raven's Coloured Progressive Matrices test* of non-verbal ability). Attainment scores in spelling and reading were also strong. A relatively weak score in *Goodenough's Draw-a-person test* stood out.

Chronological Age:	8.11	Test Age	Centile
British Picture Vocabulary Scale – 3rd Edition (Understanding Vocabulary)		10.0	80
Raven's Coloured Progressive Matrices (Non-verbal)		–	75
Vernon Spelling Test – 3rd Edition		9.10	66

Single Word Reading Test (nfer Form 1)		9.06	58
Text Reading: Neale Analysis of Reading Ability (Form 1)	Accuracy	12.10 +	93
	Comprehension	11.01	78
Goodenough Draw-a-Person (Aston Index)		7.09	–
Short Term Auditory Memory: Digit Repetition		–	50

David was referred to me because of Class Teacher's and parents' concerns regarding progress with writing: content, handwriting and spelling. A considerable discrepancy between this and performance in reading and maths had been noted.

David enjoyed school, rating his enjoyment as 5/5. He named many friends and talked about his love of playing football at play times. David highlighted his enjoyment of learning through new topics, mentioning topics on *Italy* and *the Tudors*, especially. He identified maths and reading as personal strengths, but could not, or chose not to, identify areas he found more challenging. When asked specifically to rate his feelings towards writing, David gauged this as 3/5.

He made and maintained good eye contact throughout our session and co-operated with all tasks presented. David's relatively weak score for his drawing of a person reflected issues with proportion (size of head relative to body, for example).

Standardised spelling test score outcome fell within the high average range for age at centile sixty-six. David was able to write sentences of ten plus words from dictation. He experienced no difficulty remembering these, producing the correct number of words with good spelling accuracy in context. Sometimes, he remembered full stops, but consistent use of capital letters to begin sentences was erratic.

David constructed and wrote a series of sentences about his little brother. Again, he produced the correct number of words, with entirely accurate spelling in context, but sentence structures lacked variety, all beginning in the same way, with no attempt to develop complex or compound sentences.

David used his left hand to write and usually made use of his right hand to stabilise paper. Although pencil grip and posture for writing were appropriate, David appeared to be writing from his wrist, rather than his fingers, and this impacted on pencil control. As a result, size of handwriting was irregular, letters were not well positioned on lines and spaces between words were often inadequate; writing speed was reasonable, however. When asked if he wrote with pen or pencil in class, David confirmed that he used pencil as he did not yet have a *Pen Licence*. 'You have to write *really neatly*' (to qualify).

David presented as a clearly able little boy with a number of significant strengths. My impression was that he felt quietly frustrated by his unwieldy handwriting and limited progress towards achieving the prestigious, and apparently, elusive *Pen Licence* award. Writing from his wrist may have developed as a result of being left-handed, impacting both on pencil control and the rate at which his arm tired, making writing a laborious activity, causing him to run out of steam before others, because of the increased effort required.

Approaches to Supporting Children, like Evie, Owen, Matthew and David, who experience Specific Learning Difficulties – activities and strategies that experience has shown can make a positive difference

It is important to emphasise again that what follows are not magic wands and the impact of any strategy, activity or programme will depend heavily on the rigour with which they are implemented/delivered. Remember, too, that all children are unique and there are no hard and fast rules or foolproof strategies; sometimes, it is a case of trial and error and maximising use of those that work for an individual child.

Activities to help develop targeted skills and accelerate progress

1. Increase awareness of the parts of the mouth used to articulate sounds: lips (p, b etc), tip of the tongue (t, d etc) or back of the throat (h, c etc). Encourage use of a mirror so that children can observe the parts of their mouths used to make sounds to help differentiate between these. This approach emphasises the links between articulation and pronunciation and use of phonics for decoding and encoding words.

2. Promote visual as well as phonic approaches to reading to build a sight vocabulary of high frequency words. Draw attention to the shapes of words, the number of letters etc. Challenge children to find target words within displays/in books etc.

3. Consider the *Precision Monitoring* approach (see Appendix III) which may prove a motivating technique for learning to recognise high frequency words quickly. Competition can be a great motivator and children often enjoy attempting to beat their own previous scores.

4. Consider implementing a Programme such as *Direct Phonics* (see Appendix IV) to build on and consolidate phonic knowledge.

5. Some children benefit considerably from following *The Word Wasp Hornet Literacy Primer – A Manual for Teaching the Basic Rules and Structures of English (Reading and Spelling)*; this links word articulation and pronunciation with accurate decoding (reading) and encoding (spelling) of print. As a guide, it is particularly worth consideration during Years Two and Three. *The Word Wasp Phonics and Structure Reading and Spelling Programme* is sometimes helpful for use with older children (Years Five and Six, as a general guide).

6. Encourage use of context to aid reading for meaning and use of expression by sometimes encouraging looking ahead to the next full stop, marking it with a finger and reading up to it.

7. Help with tracking lines of print, *line-by-line*, rather than *word-by-word*, to promote reading fluency; use of a ruler, a commercially produced reading *window* or even a piece of paper can support this.

8. Word searches can help with development of tracking skills, as can word or letter hunts from paragraphs and then pages – for example, tracking lines to find all the *b* letters on the page or finding the word *and* wherever it appears.

9. Before writing independently, encourage children to verbalise sentences, one at a time. Try teaching them to count the number of words they have said, producing a dash to represent each one, so that the number of words needing to be written is clear and a prompt for self-checking.

10. Good spelling and good handwriting often tend to go together and it can be useful to link the two. Encourage a cursive style of writing as soon as possible. Joined handwriting practice, involving insecure high-frequency words or a child's own repeated errors, will help to build a *motor memory* of the correct spellings. Use positive language to identify the *tricky bits*, drawing attention to what needs to be remembered. Use of coloured/special pens may help to maintain motivation. *N.B. Sometimes cursive script proves an impossible challenge; if this remains the case by Year Five, accept printing. Sometimes children come to this decision themselves after years of effort; respect personal decisions and manage your expectations.*

11. *Mnemonics* can support spelling through memory prompts, some of which are rhymes: *Don't forget the hen in when! What a hat!*

12. Include regular, short and simple dictation exercises – three sentences a few times weekly perhaps. This will give children relief from the burden of composition, allowing focus on the mechanical aspects of writing. When undertaking dictations encourage the following:

    • watch the speaker's mouth

    • repeat sentence aloud before writing it

    • repeat sentence again (whisper) simultaneously to writing it.

    Facilitate opportunities for *self-marking dictations from correctly written models*, allowing children to allocate as many ticks as possible – to each individual word written accurately and even to appropriate use of capital letters and full stops. This can be surprisingly motivating.

13. Teach handwriting through use of blue (sky), green (grass) and brown (soil) colours. *Blue sky* letters are those with ascenders that reach up to the sky, like *h*. *Green grass* letters are those without ascenders/descenders that stay in the grass at ground level, like *a*. *Brown soil* letters are those with descenders with roots that reach underground, like *g*. Always provide lined paper for writing – *try extra dark lines.*

14. The following sentence uses each letter of the alphabet at least once – *A quick brown fox jumps over the lazy dog.* It can be useful for handwriting practice. (If leaving adequate spaces between words is an issue, use of an ink stamp between words can be helpful.)

15. Facilitate opportunities for practising writing letters and numbers in chalk on a chalkboard (chalkboards are better than white boards due to resistance given and increased sensory feedback). Writing in chalk on the playground/pavement will provide similarly increased sensation.

16. When engaged in activities to develop fine motor skills, such as tracing, dot-to-dot, solving mazes and colouring, sometimes allow/encourage children to lie on their tummies propped up by their elbows – this will stabilise shoulder blades and encourage use of finger rather than arm movements. (Such activities can also help develop visual tracking skills.)

17. Winding an elastic band around a pencil shaft can help support grip and guide holding position; this is also more subtle than pencil grips. Some children find a piece of Blu-tack acts as an effective pencil grip.

18. Encourage learning touch-typing skills via programmes such as *BBC Bitesize Dance Mat Typing.*

19. Daily exercises (5 minutes daily) to promote hand and finger strength:

    Pencil Walks – Child holds the pencil using the correct grasp, i.e. between index finger and thumb with middle finger resting underneath. Child *walks* with fingers up the pencil until reaching the other end, then *walks* back down again.

    Next Step: Using a pencil with a rubber on the end, the child draws a dot on a piece of paper, then uses the technique to *walk* fingers to the rubber end, turning the pencil with writing fingers and erasing the dot. Child turns the pencil again and *walks* fingers back to the tip.

    Star Hands – Child makes a fist with one hand and stretches out the fingers of the other hand, opening and closing each hand alternately.

    Finger Slam – Child closes fingers into palms one at a time, then stretches them out, one at a time, in sequence.

    Push Hands Together – Child presses palms together with elbows pushed out sideways and holds this position for 10 seconds.

20. *Shading Boxes* – Try this activity weekly if possible. You will need paper and different coloured pencils. Draw a box 6cm by 6cm and divide it into 4 smaller boxes. Place child's hand on the page. Draw a picture or cross and ask them to keep the edge of their hand over the picture/cross whilst they colour. Ask them to colour each of the boxes in scribble of a different direction, demonstrating right diagonal scribble/left diagonal/vertical/horizontal. *N.B. The movement to shade the boxes should come from the fingers only (not the wrist or shoulder). Watch carefully. What can seem like finger movement may be a wrist movement. Remember that true, smooth efficient writing comes from finger movement only.*

21. Consider the *Basic Generic Literacy Skills Intervention Programme* at Appendix V; it combines many activities listed above and is designed to be implemented three times weekly, on a one-to-one basis, over a ten week period. Scored baseline and exit assessments are included to measure progress over time. I put this together in 2016. It was piloted extensively (school year 2016–17) by a large primary school, targeting children from Year One to Year Three. Outcomes were encouraging, with all children making measurable progress; the progress of some was particularly marked.

22. Use self-practice cards to learn number bonds to ten/twenty (pairs of numbers making ten/ twenty when added together) e.g. with six on one side and four on the other, child looks at one side and works out the number needed to make ten before turning the card over to self-check. This approach can support learning multiplication tables too.

Strategies to enhance accessibility and inclusion in the classroom and beyond

1. Consider hearing/sight checks. Hearing/vision impairments are always worth ruling out.

2. Perhaps the most empowering strategy is to arrange for *pre-teaching support before lessons*, as necessary and where possible. Going through shared texts in advance, as rehearsals, can increase the confidence of targeted children.

3. Make use of audio books. These will allow children to access age appropriate reading material, including helping to develop vocabulary and enabling associated discussions with peers capable of reading such texts independently.

4. Use *advance organisers* – put questions at the beginning of a passage instead of at the end or encourage *reading the questions first*.

5. *Minimise some* writing tasks. *Cloze Procedure* can be a useful approach, where children are required to insert missing words into sentences provided, without having to write whole sentences themselves. Getting children to build sentences by sequencing words from cut up sentences can also be useful. Using sentences they have constructed verbally can personalise the activity.

6. Request *alternative* (not written) methods of recording in areas of curriculum beyond English. (Children often become disillusioned, with reduced enjoyment of practical activities, because, 'We always have to write about it afterwards!')

7. Allow use of *post-it* notes to record/sequence ideas (in pictures perhaps). *Post-it* notes will enable ease of re-sequencing.

8. Mixed ability groups/pairs, with able scribes, will allow others less capable of scribing, to share and record good ideas, without the worry of having to write.

9. Group key/topic words together on a *key ring*, a *book mark* or a *word mat* for easy spelling reference.

10. Encourage use of interesting words even if unsure of spelling – suggest writing first sound, followed by a line for completing later.

11. Encourage children to use *invented* spelling of unfamiliar words, underlining in pencil as they go. This gives them a starting point for proof-reading.

12. Discourage use of dictionaries/wordbooks/asking adults/peers while writing first draft so that flow is not interrupted.

13. When reading through writing, *proof reading backwards from the end* can help with spotting spelling mistakes.

14. Remember that writing composition places additional load on memory, so spelling may deteriorate in context/under pressure. Be realistic and understanding.

15. Expect learned words to be spelled correctly in context – mark errors with a dot in the margin to give children a chance to spot/self-correct.

16. Promote confidence in writing by limiting spelling correction.

17. Provide resources on tables/walls to support multisensory learning e.g. alphabet strips, b/d orientation memory joggers, white boards and pens. *Cues on walls, rather than desk tops, can make reliance on these less obvious.*

18. Children should sit opposite the teacher when engaged in phonics activities and be encouraged to observe the teacher's mouth movements.

19. Consider providing a *transparent* pencil case and/or zipped wallets for books so that all items are held together and easily visible/accessible.

20. Display a chart on the classroom door/in the cloakroom with a visual checklist of what needs to be taken home. A similar chart on the bedroom door can provide a checklist of what needs to be taken to school.

21. Enable easy access to personal objects, such as coat peg, work tray and lunchbox. Locating these at the ends of rows, for example, will support accessibility.

22. Encourage *consistent* use of non-writing hand to keep paper still when writing.

23. Use of a sloped desk or Lever Arch file stuffed with newspaper (less obvious) on the desk can sometimes help to improve posture for writing.

24. Encourage writing on *alternate lines* only, as this makes work more legible/presentable. Teach the child to mark up the lines before starting. *It is important to help children present their work as well as possible so that they feel proud of it. If your work looks a mess, it can feel demoralising.*

25. Avoid copying tasks. If copying is really necessary, provide desk-top versions or copies on which children can highlight key words instead.

26. Adapt worksheets – larger print/double line spacing etc.

27. Provide pre/partly drawn diagrams, charts, graphs etc for children to complete.

28. Allow access to table squares, number lines and calculators to enable lesson participation.

29. Accept some homework in typed form if and when children become comfortable with this.

30. Sometimes, pupils with specific needs will require additional provision to be put in place so they can participate in the Key Stage One and Two National Curriculum Tests, taken in Years Two and Six respectively. These are known as *Access Arrangements*, where adjustments can be made to support pupils, for example, with reading, writing or processing difficulties. *Access Arrangements* might involve additional time, use of scribes, transcripts, and use of word processors or other technical aids. Use of readers is among the other possibilities. *Access Arrangements* should be *based on normal classroom practice.* Support given must not change the test questions and answers must be a pupil's own. Some, such as *extra time at Key Stage Two, must be applied for in advance*, unless there is an *Education, Health and Care Plan* or *Statement of SEN* in place.

Generalised/Global Learning Difficulties – insight

Children in this category typically present with relatively flat, as opposed to spikey, cognitive assessment profiles and weak performance/scores across the board. They learn at a slower pace than the majority. *Generalised Learning Difficulties* are sometimes referred to as *Global Difficulties* or *Global Developmental Delay,* where reaching all milestones is later than expected for age.

Generalised/Global Learning Difficulties are categorised on a continuum from *Moderate (MLD)* to *Severe (SLD)* through to *Profound and Multiple (PMLD).* Those with *SLD/PMLD* remain likely to attend specialist settings, while those with *MLD* are commonly found within mainstream provision. Personally, I have found the term *MLD* misleading and, at times, unhelpful over the years, particularly when helping parents/carers to understand/come to terms with their child's additional needs. The word *moderate* suggests *not too extreme*, but children described as having *MLD* often experience very significant challenges. As a general guide, cognitive assessment outcomes will be around centile two.

Generalised/Global Learning Difficulties case examples (Aleena and Anton)

Aleena

Aleena presented with Moderate Learning Difficulties (MLD). We met when she was five years, eight months and in Year One. Although physically mature in appearance, with age appropriate self-care skills, observations indicated weak social and task engagement and that there was already a wide gap at school between Aleena's functioning and that of her peers. The assessment profile below shows weak general cognitive skills (demonstrated by scored outcomes with the *British Picture Vocabulary Scale* and *Raven's Coloured Progressive Matrices* test of non-verbal ability).

Chronological Age:	5.08	Test Age	Centile
British Picture Vocabulary Scale – 3rd Edition (Understanding Vocabulary)		< 3.09	4
Raven's Coloured Progressive Matrices (non-verbal)		–	2.3

Aleena had been referred because of delayed speech, language, fine motor and social skills. Discussion with a Support Assistant, involved with Aleena since she was in Reception, gave considerable insight into her presentation at school day-to-day. She commented on inconsistencies with number/word recognition and reliable counting to ten. She also mentioned Aleena's frequent use of gesture to make herself understood. Aleena's sulking and becoming tearful when not getting her own way was also highlighted, as was her tendency to become overly possessive within friendships. Aleena's significant interest in *girly* accessories had been observed too, as had her knowledge of the related vocabulary. This is not unusual; children with considerable learning difficulties often know vocabulary of particular significance to them, where their wider knowledge is very limited.

Observation in class during a maths lesson (fourteen children and two staff) highlighted Aleena's minimal engagement. The objective was to measure with a ruler. The initial task was to measure your own hand from wrist to end of tallest finger. Aleena was encouraged to measure an adult's hand first and she engaged on a one-to-one basis. When not supported directly, she was immediately off-task, using the ruler either as a tool to mime a sawing action or as a weapon to mime sword fighting. With direct one-to-one support Aleena engaged again to measure her own hand. She said that it measured, 'four' and this was corrected to 'fourteen.'

During the *Carpet session* to discuss outcomes, Aleena played with the ruler and was not at all engaged unless continually prompted. She required one-to-one prompting to realise that she was one of three children to have the longest hand, smiling briefly, but requiring further prompting to raise her hand in recognition of this. Aleena had no apparent interest in identifying whose hand was shortest. She was unresponsive to collective instructions, such as to put rulers down and required individual prompting to respond.

During *Independent Work* (a work sheet-based activity involving estimating and then measuring the length of books with *Unifix* cubes) Aleena required one-to-one, step-by-step, prompting to collect what was needed for the task and to write her name on the sheet, which she wrote as *ALa*. She built a tower from *Unifix* cubes successfully and independently. When required to count cubes, she began at twenty and needed support with one-to-one correspondence.

Aleena had no concept of estimation, even with the excellent one-to-one support, via practical demonstration, offered. At times, she required guidance even to look in the right direction. Aleena was unable to recognise when her tower was tall enough to match the height of a particular book without having this indicated to her. She required continual, precise direction regarding where to write answers on the work sheet. Aleena wanted to look through books rather than measure them and found maintaining task focus very challenging.

During *Snack Time* she collected an apple independently from her lunchbox and sat on the carpet to eat it appropriately. She showed some interest in news others were sharing with the class, looking in the direction of the speakers from time to time.

When working on a one to one basis, beyond the classroom, Aleena was very distracted by items on the table and around the room. She was more interested in my nail polish and necklace than in engaging in conversation or tasks I initiated. Aleena commented, 'Nail polish on' as she sought to stroke my nail and later, 'I like thems' (Pointing to my necklace). When asked what she had played at play time, Aleena listed the names of children and when pressed, explained what they had played via actions rather than words. She identified a girl she considers to be her best friend.

Aleena was unable to identify anything she likes or dislikes at school, even with the support of picture cues. When asked how old she is, Aleena held up five fingers, but said, 'Ten'. She referred to *letters as numbers*. Aleena told me that she attended *phonics sessions* 'In Reception.' At times, she broke into unrecognisable speech which could only be described as *gobbledegook* to the listener. Maintenance of eye contact was erratic and fleeting. Aleena responded to smiles and a light-hearted approach, smiling broadly on occasion.

During the ***British Picture Vocabulary Scale*** assessment, Aleena required continual prompts to look at the arrays of pictures. On seeing a picture of a horse, she commented, 'Want horsey' and on seeing a spoon said, 'Look café!'

When required to give sounds to match letters, Aleena managed a few (*s, a, g, o, k, l, ss*) and accompanied these with corresponding actions. She recognised her name, along with four ***Phase 2*** words: *a, is, big* and *I*. She wrote her name as *AeL* and wrote letters, several of which were reversed, at random to match sounds.

Anton

Anton, too, presented with Moderate Learning Difficulties (MLD). Towards the end of Year Five, he had moved to the United Kingdom from Goa, having been taught through the medium of English. We met when he was ten years, seven months old, having just transferred to Year Six. The assessment profile below confirms very weak general cognitive skills (demonstrated, in particular, by scored outcomes, below centile two and, therefore, well below average with the *British Picture Vocabulary Scale* and *Raven's Coloured Progressive Matrices test* of non-verbal ability). Relatively weak short-term auditory memory score, at centile eight, will have been compounding weaknesses with understanding, having implications for retention.

Chronological Age:	10.07		Test Age	Centile
British Picture Vocabulary Scale – 3rd Edition (Understanding Vocabulary)	5.09			< 2
Raven's Coloured Progressive Matrices (Non-verbal)			–	1
Vernon Spelling Test – 3rd Edition	8.04			19
Single Word Reading Test (nfer Form 1)	8.00			14
Text Reading: Neale Analysis of Reading Ability (Form 1)	**Accuracy**		8.04	20
	Comprehension		6.07	1
Short Term Auditory Memory: Digit Repetition			–	8

Anton had been referred by his Class Teacher who queried the limitations of his cognitive skills. She had observed very weak mathematical understanding, but ability to recite tables, having learned these by rote, with no concept of their meaning.

When working on a *one-to-one basis,* Anton co-operated with all tasks, presenting as polite and well-mannered. He responded well to specific praise regarding his neat handwriting, thanking me when I complimented him. Handwriting was neat, well-formed and of uniform size. Anton's use of spoken language reflected limitations. When asked about activities he enjoys at playtimes, for example, he said, 'Today, with my friends, football.'

His scores for spelling and reading accuracy were markedly higher than cognitive assessment outcomes, falling towards or just within the low average range for his age. Text reading comprehension score, at *centile one*, alongside text reading accuracy score at *centile twenty*, however, highlighted the significant gap between ability to decode and understand texts.

Anton's earlier education seemed to have prioritised rote learning, enabling the development of reasonable mechanical literacy and numeracy skills; relative success in these areas can sometimes mask other limitations. Beyond this, the demands of a wider curriculum, emphasising different priorities and styles of teaching and learning, highlighted gaps that in previous setting would have been much less obvious.

Approaches to supporting children, like Aleena and Anton, who experience Generalised/Global Learning Difficulties – activities and strategies that experience has shown can make a positive difference

It is important to emphasise again that what follows are not magic wands and the impact of any strategy, activity or programme will depend heavily on the rigour with which they are implemented/delivered. Remember, too, that all children are unique and there are no hard and fast rules or foolproof strategies; sometimes, it is a case of trial and error and maximising use of those that work for an individual child.

Activities to help develop basic skills and accelerate progress

1. *Backward Chaining* is probably the single most helpful technique that I have come across. It can be applied to a range of tasks from life skills, such as bed-making to self-care skills such as dressing (including learning to tie shoelaces) to letter/number formation, to learning to write one's own name and spelling other words.

   Backward Chaining involves *breaking down the steps of a task and teaching these in reverse order.* Instead of the child starting at the beginning and getting lost some way through, with the adult having to complete the task, the adult does all but the last step and *lets the child complete the work*, ensuring immediate success and satisfaction.

   Gradually, the adult fades back, doing fewer and fewer steps, while *the child does more and more*, always ending with the child performing the final step.

   An example of support with learning to put on a jumper might be illustrated as follows:

   Step 1 Assist checking jumper is not inside out.

   Step 2 Assist checking position of label to identify back and front.

   Step 3 Assist putting arm through one sleeve.

   Step 4 Assist putting other arm through other sleeve.

   Step 5 Assist putting head through the appropriate opening.

   Step 6 Child pulls the jumper down into position independently.

   The first time you would assist with steps 1–5, encouraging independent completion of step 6.

   Next time, you would assist with steps 1–4, encouraging independent completion of steps 5 and 6 and so on until the child is achieving independently.

2. The emphasis on phonics to teach reading and spelling in recent years has limited visual, whole word approaches. Children with global learning difficulties often do much better with the latter; some find phonics impossible. Try whole word, *visual rather than phonic*, approaches to reading. **Precision Monitoring** (see Appendix III) can be helpful here.

3. **Precision Monitoring** can also help with number recognition and increasing accuracy and confidence with number bonds.

4. Help children to notice simple words when out and about (in/out signs at car parks etc) and numbers (on doors/buses etc); single digit numbers in the first instance.

5. If struggling to spell their name, try use of different colours to section parts for increased visual impact: A-**lee**-na.

6. Provide opportunities to *walk* the shapes of large versions of letters and numbers, written on the ground in chalk, to help embed correct starting points and accurate formation. Get child to walk, hop or jump the shape of the letter or number, always ensuring beginning at the correct point. This activity could prove enjoyable with family on the beach, drawing letters and numbers in damp sand instead.

7. Drawing shapes on the ground in chalk is another possibility. Call out the shapes, at random, encouraging the child to stand on the appropriate one.

8. If colour recognition is inconsistent, parents/carers might think about having a weekly *colour focus*, helping to gather and display collections of perhaps ten items from around the home.

9. Consider programmes such as **Plus 1 (The Introductory Coaching System for Maths Success)** and **Power of 2 (The Coaching System for Maths Success)** to help understanding, retention and confidence with number. *Little and often* is best, rather than longer, less frequent sessions: ten minutes, on a one-to-one basis, three to five times weekly is ideal. The programmes are straightforward to implement as no additional resources are needed, beyond the book and a pencil. They can be of benefit to those who require repeated practice, explanation and opportunities for consolidation.

10. Consider further programmes in the same series, such as **Perform with Times Tables (The One-to-one Coaching System for Success with Multiplication and Division)** and **Perform with Time (The One-to-one Coaching System for Success with Time)**.

11. The multisensory nature of **Numicon** materials makes these particularly appropriate for those who require additional support with retention and application of number concepts.

12. Children are often well motivated by LDA's **Stile** and **Starter Stile** resources, a range of Literacy and Numeracy based workbooks for use with the **Stile** Tray/**Stile Starter** Tray. The self-checking activities give children a feeling of autonomy and involve placing numbered tiles on appropriate squares on the base of the tray. When all tiles have been placed, children close the tray, turn it over, and reopen it to reveal a geometric pattern. If the answers are all correct, the pattern will match the one printed at the top of the exercise.

The activities provide a different way of practising and consolidating the same skills. Variety of approach is welcome and useful for maintaining interest and motivation.

13. Increased emphasis on *functional maths* skills is likely to prove particularly helpful to personal confidence: for example adequate understanding of time and money. By Year Five, limiting accuracy and understanding with telling the time *digitally*, beyond analogue clocks, can be helpful to avoid sending children into panic mode. *Embedding the concept of time through visual timelines can be useful.*

14. *Give a commentary* while engaged in practical activities, such as cooking or art and craft, to generate language links and reinforce processes.

Strategies to enhance accessibility and inclusion in the classroom and beyond

1. Consider hearing/sight checks. Hearing/vision impairments are always worth ruling out.

2. Perhaps the most empowering strategy is to arrange for *pre-teaching support before lessons*, as necessary and where possible. Preparing for lessons *in advance, as rehearsals*, can increase the confidence of targeted children.

3. Introducing a range of methods in maths, to arrive at the same outcomes, can be unhelpful and add to confusion; sometimes, teaching and learning *just one method* supports confidence and retention.

4. Use of visual timetables as augmentative means of communication can prove supportive both at school and at home.

5. Display a chart on the classroom door/in the cloakroom with a visual checklist of what needs to be taken home. A similar chart on the bedroom door can provide a checklist of what needs to be taken to school.

6. Provide visual back-up to spoken language using gesture and demonstration as much as possible, as well as use of symbols and pictures. *Show as well as tell!*

7. Break instructions down into short simple steps, using words and actions to clarify sequence: first, next, last.

8. Include and support in questioning by offering a limited choice of answers. Instead of asking 'What shape is this?' try 'Is this shape a square or a rectangle?'

9. When questioning, discourage others from *answering targeted questions (or interrupting)*. Allow *thinking time* before prompting (count to 5 in your head) and offer *to come back later*. As children get older and become more self-aware, avoiding eye contact can reduce pressure at this time.

10. Check for understanding regularly – *beyond repeating,* ask children to explain (*tell you in their own words*) or, *where possible, show their understanding through practical demonstration*.

11. Request *alternative* (not written) methods of recording in areas of curriculum beyond English. Children often become disillusioned, with reduced enjoyment of practical activities, because, 'We always have to write about it afterwards!'

12. Allow use of *post-it* notes to record/sequence ideas (in pictures perhaps). *Post-it* notes will enable ease of re-sequencing.

13. Mixed ability groups/pairs, with able scribes, will allow inclusion of the less able, without the worry of having to write.

14. Group key/topic words together on a *key ring*, a *book mark* or a *word mat* for easy reading/ spelling reference.

15. Provide resources on tables/walls to support multisensory learning e.g. alphabet strips, *b/d* orientation memory joggers, white boards and pens. *Cues on walls, rather than desk tops can make reliance on these less obvious.*

16. Provide pre/partly drawn diagrams, charts, graphs etc for children to complete.

Section 2
Communication and Interaction

During the early years of schooling, there is much emphasis on speaking and listening skills to develop understanding and use of language; these are vital, not only for effective social interaction and general engagement, but ultimately for providing a foundation for reading comprehension and ability to formulate sentences for writing. Inability to communicate a message using spoken language will impact on ability to compose in writing.

Children from language-rich homes have an advantage and, unless they have a particular learning difficulty, often arrive at school with much wider vocabularies than peers from homes where language use is more limited. In recent years, this advantage may have been eroded to some extent as a result of increased use of technology. Where face-to-face speaking, listening and social interaction were once priorities, access to tablets, phones and other devices has changed the nature of communication and reduced time available for direct personal engagement.

Children with particular needs in this category experience challenges communicating with others; they are described as having *Speech, Language and Communication Needs (SLCN)*. Some have issues expressing what they want to say because of speech-sound development and poor speech clarity. Others struggle with talking and ability to join words to form sentences using the correct vocabulary and grammar; this is known as difficulty with *expressive* language. Some children may have limitations with understanding what is said; this is described as difficulty with *receptive* language. Other children struggle to understand and/or use the rules of social communication; some may have a diagnosis of an *Autism Spectrum Disorder*.

As with *Cognition and Learning* (Section One), children with needs in this category fall into two groups: those with *Specific Language Impairment/Language Disorder* and those experiencing *General Language Impairment/Delay*. Some teachers question the need to differentiate between the two groups, maintaining that both benefit from similar approaches and, arguably, this is true; hence, the supportive activities and strategies listed are appropriate for both groups. Given the frequency with which children are identified, formally or informally, as struggling with aspects of social communication, this has been presented as an additional, discrete category within this section.

Where English is an additional language, other considerations should be pursued to establish whether there are language barriers beyond this. Establishing, as far as possible, a child's *first language competence* with parents/carers (both receptive and expressive language) can be a useful first step. Administering an assessment tool such as the ***British Picture Vocabulary Scale*** *in both English and the child's first language* will allow comparisons between *raw score* outcomes (total number of correct responses). Help with this can be sought from bilingual or multilingual staff and volunteers. *Attempts to standardise the raw score achieved in another language would be entirely inappropriate, the assessment having been based on English vocabulary and standardised according to English norms.* When children are new on roll it is also important to research the extent of any previous school or pre-school experience within other English settings, if this is not already known; this will give useful information regarding the extent of previous exposure to the English language.

Any hearing loss, or history of this, can also have significant implications for progress and result in delayed language development. Commonly occurring conditions, such as *Glue Ear*, can cause intermittent hearing loss which requires on-going monitoring. Where this is the sole barrier, and there is no specific language impairment or weak cognitive ability, children can often progress quickly to age-related expectations once this is addressed with appropriate support.

Specific Language Impairment (SLI)/Language Disorder – insight

Sometimes, children are described as having a Specific Language Impairment or a Language Disorder, where one or more aspects of language development are weak in relation to others and/or general cognitive ability. For example, a child may present with unintelligible speech, but age appropriate receptive language (understanding) and expressive language (use of appropriate spoken vocabulary and sentence construction). A different child may struggle with *expressive* language but demonstrate age appropriate *receptive* language. Occasionally, apparently effective *expressive* language will mask weak *receptive* language, with children managing to use a range of learned phrases/sentences in correct context, yet with little understanding.

Speech and language therapists are often very interested in children's non-verbal assessment outcomes (such as those achieved with **Raven's Matrices** – see Appendix I). High scores here, contrasted with weak language scores, can also indicate a Specific Language Impairment/ Disorder. Indeed, speech and language therapy is often only provided to children in mainstream schools who have Specific rather than General Language Impairment. This is on the basis that these children are considered more capable of making significant progress, learning to implement self-supportive strategies and generalise their learning more readily and independently, as a result of their higher cognitive ability. Where Specific Language Impairment/Disorder is suspected, referral to a Speech and Language Therapist for detailed specialist assessment and advice is, therefore, very important.

Specific Language Impairment/Language Disorder case examples (Benjamin, Rya and Tomasz)

Benjamin (English is home and sole language)

Benjamin presented with likely Specific Language Impairment at an early stage. We met when he was five years, six months and in a Reception class. On transfer from school's Nursery he had been described as very able, with an apparently photographic memory; this was largely because he had acquired excellent knowledge of letters and their corresponding sounds (phonics) and had learned to read a number of whole words, by sight, with automatic recall. Benjamin's Reception Class Teacher reported significant concerns, however, regarding his language skills and receptive language (understanding) in particular.

Benjamin's assessment profile (see below) was very uneven/spikey: robust non-verbal ability and reading accuracy (demonstrated by scored outcomes with *Raven's Coloured Progressive Matrices, Neale Analysis of Reading Ability accuracy* score and *NFER Single Word Reading Test*) alongside significant, specific difficulties with understanding receptive vocabulary and reading comprehension, relative to reading accuracy (demonstrated by scored outcomes with *British Picture Vocabulary Scale* and *Neale Analysis of Reading Ability comprehension* score).

Chronological Age:	5.06		Test Age	Centile
British Picture Vocabulary Scale – 3rd Edition			<3.09	5
Raven's Coloured Progressive Matrices (Non-verbal)			–	83
Text Reading: Neale Analysis of Reading Ability (Form 1)	Accuracy		6.05	N/A - too young for standardised scoring
	Comprehension		<6.01	
Single Word Reading: NFER – Graded Word Reading Test (Form 1)			6.03	78

Observation in class demonstrated willingness to take turns and persevere with practical, drawing and play-based tasks. He was able to maintain appropriate sitting at a table, applying an effective, right-handed pencil grip with good pencil control.

Benjamin responded accordingly to regular and familiar instructions linked to the daily routine, such as when his name was called during registration or when everyone was told to get ready to go outside. Conversely, Benjamin was more uncertain when required to follow less routine instructions and struggled to locate paper, even with one-to-one direction. Although a willing participant when engaged with the Class Teacher on a one-to-one basis, Benjamin required targeted use of closed questions with optional answers provided to direct and support his responses.

When playing with a train and cars, as one of a group of six, Benjamin's verbal interaction was minimal and he remained apparently in a world of his own, engaging in parallel, rather than interactive play. During outside play, he tended to initiate and engage in conversation more with adults than with children. Benjamin was observed to seek and maintain appropriate eye contact. Play was quite physical, at times, with Benjamin involved in play-fighting, stopping this when becoming aware of an adult supervisor observing. At other times, he charged around the playground, both on his own and as part of a group.

Benjamin seemed popular with peers who sought to include him, encouraging his involvement in a game of *Chase. Interestingly, when playing, peers were heard to give very precise, closed instructions, preceded by his name, such as, 'Benjamin! Get him!'* They had obviously recognised Benjamin's need for targeted direction when participating in a game.

Engagement with me on a one-to-one basis was immediate, with Benjamin making and maintaining good eye contact. Although he seemed to enjoy chatting, his speech was often unintelligible, even when the context was known. Benjamin was unable to pronounce the sound of the letter *s*, for example, hence *school* became *dool* and *supersonic, duperdonic*.

Discussion with Benjamin confirmed that he knew his age, but not his birthday and when asked, he told me something like, 'My birthday in the dool.' Benjamin identified his favourite toy at school as 'Blue Donic' (Blue Sonic). Favourite toys at home were cars, 'I play cars and I win.'

Responses in conversation often reflected weak comprehension and use of language. For example, when asked what makes him feel happy at school, he responded, 'And my he going to be happy with teacher if writing good.' When asked if he ever feels sad at school, he responded, 'When you cry and your friend and he *day* hit head . . . . and . . . and . . . He . . . Fighting . . . now he cries.'

Benjamin was able to read many high-frequency words (most **Phase 2–5** words listed at Appendix II). *He had instant recall of these without the need to decode with phonic strategies (use letter sounds to support word-building).* Benjamin knew most **Phase 2** and **3** letter sounds in isolation but did not rely on use of these to read through a set of three letter *consonant, vowel, consonant* words, such as *ham*, *sit* and *leg*; instead, he relied on visual recall, managing to read 18/25. Benjamin was similarly successful with a range of four and five letter words, incorporating initial and/or final *consonant blends*, such as *ch*in, *cra*sh and wi*sh*, managing to read 18/25 words again. *Standardised reading assessment* outcome scores for both text and single word reading *accuracy* fell within the high average range for age but, as expected, comprehension lagged significantly.

Benjamin was able to write letters to match most single letter sounds, often writing the capital letter first, followed by the lowercase when this was requested. He was usually able to spell *vowel consonant* and *consonant, vowel, consonant* words, such as *it* and *sat*, accurately. Benjamin's pencil control was good and he made consistent use of his non-writing left hand to stabilise paper and posture when drawing and writing. Letter formation was clear and assured and he was confident when writing his first name. Benjamin made a good attempt at writing the sentence – *I like playing cars* and showed awareness of word boundaries, producing four words, adequately spaced, and adding a full stop when asked what was needed at the end of his sentence.

Further assessment of receptive vocabulary (understanding) with the **British Picture Vocabulary Scale** confirmed *weak comprehension with an outcome score at age equivalent below three years, nine months and percentile five* (within the moderately below average range for his age). The following are examples of words he did not yet understand: toe, belt, fence, hook, calendar, feather and desk.

In contrast, Benjamin's non-verbal assessment score (**Raven's Coloured Matrices**) was high and he achieved a standardised score at *percentile eighty three* (the very top end of the high average range for his age), having made careful and considered choices.

Rya (home language is not known for sure)

Rya presented with a very uneven assessment profile, demonstrating likely Specific Language Impairment/Disorder. We met when she was eight years, five months and in Year Four. Rya's standardised assessment outcomes (see below) indicated robust non-verbal ability and short-term auditory memory (demonstrated by scored outcomes with *Raven's Progressive Coloured Matrices* and *Digit*

Repetition Test of Short-term Auditory Memory). These outcomes are in stark contrast to that achieved for receptive vocabulary (demonstrated by *British Picture Vocabulary Scale* score). Traits of dyslexia, associated with very weak spelling relative to other areas of personal strength, are also noteworthy.

Chronological Age:	8.05	Test Age	Centile
British Picture Vocabulary Scale – 3rd Edition (Understanding Vocabulary)		5.00	< 2
Raven's Coloured Progressive Matrices (Non-verbal)		–	95
Vernon Spelling Test – 3rd Edition		–	< 2
Single Word Reading Test (nfer Form 1)		7.09	30
Text Reading: Neale Analysis of Reading Ability (Form 1)	Accuracy	7.09	37
	Comprehension	7.09	30
Short Term Auditory Memory: Digit Repetition		–	50

Rya's case is particularly interesting as it illustrates how lack of continuity can hinder appropriate educational provision and outcomes for any child, but especially the more vulnerable. She was new on roll in Year Four and this was her *third* primary school.

Interestingly and coincidentally, I had met Rya previously when she was in a Reception class at her first school. At that time, school had raised concerns regarding unusual behaviours, including aggressive interaction with peers and some echolalia (repetition of utterances heard). It had been observed that Mum spoke little English and had not disclosed Rya's first language. By Year One she had left her first school and I was intrigued to meet up with her again in Year Four. *It was very disappointing to learn that no school records had been forwarded, despite these having been persistently pursued.*

Rya had been on roll for five months when school sought my involvement because of concerns regarding unusual social behaviours such as laughing at inappropriate times, and weak spelling. School also reported some interesting strengths, describing Rya as an apparently confident girl who could be quite creative and surprisingly insightful on occasion.

Observation within a mixed ability class setting, where children were discussing characters from Roald Dahl's book *Fantastic Mr Fox*, highlighted Rya's willingness to answer questions asked of the class. She raised her hand to volunteer a response and when chosen, described *appearance rather than personality traits,* as had been requested. Rya did not engage in task-related interaction with her neighbour, when asked to discuss Mr Fox's character with a partner, and eventually challenged him to an arm wrestle instead. She described Mr Fox as *curious* when asked directly by the class teacher, but was unable to explain why.

During one-to-one work Rya tended to go off at tangents in conversation. She rated her enjoyment of school at that time as 5/5, but could not verbalise reasons. Rya reported that she was happy to leave her previous school, 'People bullied me. They thought me and Jack were in love cos we always played together and we didn't have other friends.'

According to Rya she moved schools as, 'Dad was a soldier. He's a police officer now. We're going to move house again soon.' *(Rya left the school mid-way through year five.)* She mentioned her enjoyment of art lessons, 'It's fun and creative. To be honest, I like painting.' Rya believed she had friends, but not many, 'I'm not the best person of making friends. I don't really know which person to trust when I move to a new school.' When asked about activities beyond school, Rya told me, 'I'm a Muslim and Muslims are very strict. I go to Auntie's house to pray every day, five till six. On Fridays I have to do something and if I don't learn it by the time I'm ten I will go to *Hell.* I do not know how to speak Arabic. My Mum's trying to teach me Urdu, but I was born in England and I speak English.'

British Picture Vocabulary Scale score, *at below centile two and age equivalent five years*, is very weak. Rya was unable to identify pictures to match the following words, for example: map, package, island, hook, target or elbow (neither was she able to identify her own elbow).

Standardised spelling test score outcome was also very weak, at *below centile two and well below* the average range for age. Rya demonstrated significant confusion with orientation of the letters *b* and *d* and also reversed the orientation of the letter *y* in her name.

In contrast, **Raven's Coloured Progressive Matrices** (non-verbal activity) outcome score was very good at *centile ninety five*. Rya reported finding this task 'easy' and sailed through it.

Rya's own comments regarding learning Urdu gave a sense of the frustration she was feeling because of her specific difficulties with acquisition of language skills. Rya is an example of one of those children sometimes able to remember and use learned words and phrases in correct contexts, but usually with minimal understanding; without further probing, this can be misleading and go unnoticed.

Tomasz (home language is Polish)

Tomasz presented with a very uneven/spikey assessment profile which in other cases might be indicative of Specific Language Impairment/Language Disorder. We met when he was five years, four months old and in a Reception class. Tomasz' assessment profile (see below) suggested robust non-verbal ability and broadly age-appropriate drawing (demonstrated by scored outcomes with *Raven's Coloured Progressive Matrices* and his drawing of a person). In contrast, understanding of English vocabulary (demonstrated by scored outcome with the *British Picture Vocabulary Scale*) was very weak.

Chronological Age:	5.04	Test Age	Centile
British Picture Vocabulary Scale – 3rd Edition		<3.09	2
Raven's Coloured Progressive Matrices (Non-verbal)		–	50
Goodenough Draw-a-Person		5.0	–

Tomasz had arrived six months previously, at the beginning of the Reception Year, having not attended the School's Nursery or any other pre-school English setting. Reception Class Teacher noted slow progress, despite his Autumn Birthday, making him one of the older children within the year group. She queried the possibility of Cognition and Learning difficulties, beyond his more obvious needs associated with having English as an additional language.

Tomasz engaged with me immediately on a one-to-one basis, making good eye contact, smiling at appropriate times and co-operating with all tasks presented.

He identified two friends at school, both Polish. Despite willingness to engage, he was hesitant in conversation and required encouragement to speak. Tomasz told me that he had a little brother and when asked if he had a sister too replied, 'Yeah, Mum.' Offering Tomasz a range of optional responses in conversation helped give him confidence to speak. Similarly, Tomasz required considerable encouragement to draw a picture of himself, apparently because he did not understand the task. He did not appear to understand the word *drawing* and needed visual demonstration back-up to clarify verbal instructions. Once the nature of the task was understood, Tomasz produced a drawing with age appropriate detail.

Further standardised assessment of receptive vocabulary (understanding) with the ***British Picture Vocabulary Scale*** confirmed the extent of his weak comprehension with an outcome score at *age equivalent below three years, nine months and percentile two* (well below the average range for his age in comparison with others for whom English is their home, and usually sole, language). The following are examples of words he did not yet understand: belt, empty, glass, dancing, nest, rectangle and elbow. *Informal repetition of this assessment in Polish* (with the help of a Polish Teaching Assistant) allowed Tomasz to demonstrate his much wider and more age appropriate understanding of Polish words. As mentioned previously, attempts to standardise the score would be inappropriate, the assessment having been based on English vocabulary and standardised according to English norms; the outcome, nonetheless, suggests competence in understanding Polish vocabulary, making a suggestion of a Specific Language Impairment/Disorder less appropriate. *Slower than expected progress is much more likely to be largely as a result of being within the early stages of learning English as an additional language.* Tomasz' good non-verbal assessment score (**Raven's Coloured Matrices**), where a standardised score at *percentile fifty* (the mid average range for his age) was achieved, reinforces this.

Beyond these, Tomasz demonstrated his gradual acquisition of phonic knowledge, giving sounds to match most single letters from **Phases 2** and **3** (see Appendix II), making regular, self-supportive use of corresponding actions taught as a memory aid. He was also able to recognise his name and twelve other **Phase 2** high frequency words, including three *tricky* words by sight.

Tomasz was confident in writing his first name, producing well-formed letters, and managed to write letters to match twelve sounds accurately. He was able to write three of the twelve high-frequency words he could read: *Mum, Dad* and *I.* At times, Tomasz preferred to make no attempt, rather than have a go.

Although it seems unlikely that Tomasz experiences Specific Language Impairment/Disorder, children presenting in this way remain likely to benefit from similar supportive activities and strategies.

General Language Impairment/
Language Delay – insight

Sometimes, children are described as having General Language Impairment or Language Delay, demonstrating weaknesses with all aspects of speech and language. Weak language skills are often in line with weak general cognitive ability, manifested by weak non-verbal assessment outcomes (such as those achieved with **_Raven's Matrices_** – see Appendix I). Despite this, the same activities and strategies, listed later in this section, are appropriate for use with these children. Progress made is likely to be slower and personal implementation of self-supportive strategies weaker than among those experiencing Specific Language Impairment.

Children in this category present in similar ways to those identified as experiencing Generalised/Global Learning Difficulties (see Section One); hence, some of the activities recommended may also be helpful to children identified as experiencing General Language Impairment/Language Delay.

General Language Impairment/Language Delay case example (Mariam)

Mariam (home language is Punjabi)

Mariam presented with likely General Language Impairment. We met when she was three years, nine months and in the Nursery Class.

Nursery Teacher had several concerns regarding Mariam's delayed responses and *glazed eye* appearance, suggesting lack of comprehension. Teaching Assistant overseeing Mariam's group spoke fluent English and Punjabi. She reported using both languages to initiate interaction with Mariam during group activities and on a one-to-one basis; Mariam remained similarly unresponsive when communication was initiated in either language.

Observations in the Nursery Class setting confirmed Mariam's lack of engagement during a whole class phonics-based activity. Responses to joining in with collective actions were markedly delayed. When playing, interaction with other children was negligible and Mariam tended to drift from activity to activity, lingering only fleetingly. She initiated some non-verbal interaction with familiar adults in Nursery, offering toy foods which the adult pretended to eat. When playing outside, Mariam favoured the slide, climbing up and sliding down repeatedly on her own.

One-to-one assessment confirmed Mariam's weak understanding of English vocabulary (demonstrated by the scored outcome with ***British Picture Vocabulary Scale*** shown below). Where no/incorrect responses were made to English words, words and instructions were repeated in Punjabi with the help of the Punjabi speaking Teaching Assistant. *This made minimal difference (+one point) to Mariam's raw score (total number of correct responses).* She understood the word *mouth* in Punjabi but not English.

Chronological Age:	3.09	Test Age	Centile
British Picture Vocabulary Scale Assessment Outcome (3rd Edition)		<3.09	<2

Mariam achieved a raw score of just fourteen. Awareness that to achieve an age equivalent score of three years, nine months, a raw score of fifty four is needed assists contextual understanding of Mariam's very weak performance in both Punjabi and English.

Assessment and observations suggest the possibility of General Language Impairment with its implications for social interaction and engagement in Nursery and beyond. In order to reach this conclusion, access to a Punjabi speaker was essential to allow for a judgement on Mariam's competence in her home language.

Approaches to supporting children, like Rya, Benjamin, Tomasz and Mariam, who may experience Specific or General Language Impairment – activities and strategies that experience has shown can make a positive difference

It is important to emphasise again that what follows are not magic wands and the impact of any strategy, activity or programme will depend heavily on the rigour with which they are implemented/delivered. Remember, too, that all children are unique and there are no hard and fast rules or foolproof strategies; sometimes, it is a case of trial and error and maximising use of those that work for an individual child.

Activities to help develop targeted skills and accelerate progress

Commercially produced programmes or interventions can prove helpful, but it is important to observe whether programme-based learning has been generalised to impact on success rates within mainstream lessons and beyond. In other words, is the child using and applying the knowledge and skills acquired independently? Besides these, many activities can be undertaken on an *ad hoc* or incidental basis at school or beyond.

1. Consider an intervention such as *Communication Fix: An activity programme to improve children's communication skills*. This is time limited and for use with individuals or small groups (maximum of four children). There are six sections: sentence construction, vocabulary, questions, prepositions (words associated with *position*, for example, *in*, *on*, *under*), instructions and sequencing. The Programme includes pre-assessments, to help identify priority areas, and post assessments, to help measure impact.

2. *Giving a commentary* while engaged in practical activities such as cooking or art and craft allows the activity to reinforce the language. At home, engage child in helping with *routine jobs on the car/in the house/in the garden and talk about what you are doing as you do it.* Tasks might be as straightforward as pairing socks, sorting clean laundry into piles belonging to different family members, watering plants or polishing the car. Whilst it can be quicker for parents/carers to do these tasks unaided, they can provide valuable learning opportunities, particularly if you discuss the processes at the same time.

3. *Seek and Find* Ask the child to bring you things by giving either item names or descriptions, for example, 'Bring me a coin' or 'Bring me something round.'

4. *Draw from instructions* Provide children with paper and pencil and have a picture in mind (or one in front of you) that you would like them to create, having listened to and followed your instructions. Children must not be able to see the picture. Give instructions as to what to place where, for example, 'Draw a tree in the middle of the page. Draw three birds flying above the tree' etc. Alternatively, consider commercially available *fuzzy felt* boards with a range of objects to arrange in place.

5. *Gather a variety of everyday objects with children* Spread these out on a table. Can they find the one that you use for eating, wearing etc? Extend this activity by introducing two cuddly toys or dolls. Ask child to 'Give Bear the cup' or 'Give Otter the pencil.' *If repetition is needed, repeat the whole phrase rather than break it down.* Use cuddly toys also for practising understanding and using words *associated with position.* Ask child to 'Sit Bear *on* the chair' or 'Sit Bear *next to* Otter' or 'Put Otter *in* the box.'

6. *Actions to follow* Give child two to three actions to follow, for example, 'Touch your head and then tap your shoulders.' or 'Clap your hands, touch your ears, then jump up.' Support verbal instructions initially and intermittently over a longer period if required by performing the actions as you say them.

7. *I Spy* Play variations of this well-known game – 'I spy something round or something that cuts or something with legs' etc.

8. Use commercially produced or self-assembled *Story Sacks* to support understanding and re-telling stories. Items in the sacks accompany the stories, adding a tactile dimension to reinforcing meaning and bringing the tales to life.

9. *Name Three Things* Take turns to say three animals/body parts/fruits etc. Make this more challenging – take turns to say three zoo/farm/household pet animals or three parts of a leg or arm/six parts of a face or three green/red fruits etc. Other suggestions for categories: forms of transport, vegetables, clothes, furniture.

10. *Chain Game* Take turns to link each word to the last one e.g. Strawberry – fruit – raspberry – red – danger – fire – smoke – barbecue – sausages – mash etc.

11. *What could it be?* Use a selection of objects in a bag. One child takes an object without others seeing and describes it for others to guess. If unsure, encourage questions such as – Where do you find it? What do you use it for?

12. *Crosswords/Word Puzzles* Children have to think of possible words from clues.

13. *Instruct me!* Ask a child to explain in words how to do something, such as making a Mother's Day card or something they have had recent experience of making themselves. Put out the equipment and request others to carry out the process as it is explained. This will give important feedback regarding the need for a specific order.

14. *Carry on the Story* Start off a story and stop at strategic points for children to take over. Begin with familiar stories before attempting to make up own.

15. *Play Charades* Take turns to guess each other's action in order to work on *the present tense and create questions*, for example,

'You are brushing your hair.'

'Are you pushing a buggy?'

'Are you making a cup of tea?'

Strategies to enhance accessibility and inclusion in the classroom and beyond

1. Hearing tests are always worthwhile to rule out hearing impairment as a potential barrier to development of speech, language and communication. Where hearing loss has been identified, on-going monitoring will be required.

2. Beyond supporting use and understanding of language directly, give special recognition to personal strengths. Good non-verbal ability suggests likelihood of skill with activities involving spatial awareness, such as designing and making and solving visual puzzles etc. Success with these is likely to impact on general engagement, wider motivation, progress and social inclusion.

3. Where speech clarity is an issue, limit the number of contacts with whom the child needs to communicate in class; placement with the same group of peers for most of the day will allow these children to become familiar with speech patterns. This can minimise frustration experienced by challenged children, supporting their efforts in making themselves understood.

4. Provide visual back-up to spoken language using gesture and demonstration as much as possible, as well as use of symbols and pictures. *Show as well as tell!*

5. Break instructions down into short simple steps, using words and actions to clarify sequence: *first*, *next*, *last*.

6. Include and support in questioning by offering a limited choice of answers. Instead of asking 'What shape is this?' try 'Is this shape a square or a rectangle?'

7. When questioning, discourage others from *answering targeted questions (or interrupting)*. Allow *thinking time* before prompting (count to five in your head) and offer *to come back later*. As children get older and become more self-aware, avoiding eye contact can reduce pressure at this time.

8. Check for understanding regularly – *beyond repeating*, ask children to explain *(tell you in their own words) or, where possible, show their understanding through practical demonstration.*

9. Encourage self-help strategies, as necessary, to make children aware of methods that help them, *such as asking for clarification, admitting when they have lost the thread or visualisation of language heard* (turn spoken words into *mind* pictures).

10. Be aware that some children with very weak vocabularies sometimes learn the *tricks* of answering reading comprehension questions correctly, yet with little understanding. They might identify the key words in a question and locate the appropriate response by finding the same key words within a reading passage. Further probing questions can demonstrate a complete lack of understanding despite gaining the *correct answer*.

11. Use of visual timetables as alternative, augmentative means of communication can prove supportive both at school and at home.

12. *Perhaps the most effective and empowering inclusive strategy is to arrange for pre-teaching (word meanings) of subject specific key words prior to introducing new topics.* This can be done as a class, within groups or on a one-to-one basis to give targeted children a head start – make them experts even! Post/plenary teaching sessions can serve to consolidate vocabulary. Supportive parents can play a particularly useful role here, helping to cement and embed new vocabulary in advance of and even after new topics.

13. Where use of language is inadequate, model back, by repeating corrected and expanded versions of children's speech, without commenting directly on any errors. *Never expect repetition of your version, but children may echo of their own accord which is fine.*

14. Do not pretend you have understood when you have not. Where possible, ask children *to show as well as tell you.*

15. Pair with good language role models where and when possible/practical.

Social Communication Difficulties/Autism Spectrum Disorders (ASD) – insight

Children with this *medical diagnosis* range on a spectrum from the high-functioning and cognitively able, to those with more severe and/or generalised cognitive needs. Some may have needs requiring long-term specialised support and are likely to attend specialist settings; others experience fewer, yet specific needs and can be supported and included within mainstream provision.

The main areas of difficulty are associated with social interaction and communication which impact on ability to form and develop relationships. Instinctive responses to non-verbal forms of communication, such as facial expressions and eye contact, are often limited. There is also a tendency to take things literally, with little understanding of social banter. Use of language can be random and out of context, even when language skills are well developed; comments can be unwittingly, yet rudely, frank. Given that there is already scope for cross-cultural misunderstanding, having English as an additional language may complicate the process of assessment and diagnosis.

Children with an autism also frequently develop restricted, but intensely pursued interests; viewed positively, this can mean that they become experts in their specialist subjects, but viewed more negatively it can become their favoured, persistently raised topic of conversation, regardless of the interests of other children. Sometimes, sensory issues impact on behaviours. Some children become overwhelmed by over-sensitivity to sounds, touch, tastes, smells, light or colours that go unnoticed by others. Conversely, some may be under-sensitive and engage in self-stimulatory, repeated behaviours, such as hand-flapping.

Many children demonstrate some of these traits, without formal diagnosis but, diagnosis or not, the same activities and supportive strategies can prove helpful. It could be that increasing numbers are growing up less able to read people's body language or facial expressions because, when out and about on journeys and in public places, they spend little time *people-watching*. Instead of looking around in cafes, at airports or train stations, for example, many people are absorbed by technology, their eyes glued to a mobile phone or other device.

Social Communication Difficulties/Autism Spectrum Disorders case examples (Harry and Joe)

Harry (English is home and sole language)

We met when Harry was four years, seven months and about to transfer from the Nursery to Reception. He had a diagnosis of Autism Spectrum Disorder and school sought advice on including Harry and meeting his needs within the Reception Class.

Observation in Nursery during *Snack Time* demonstrated good self-help skills. Harry sat at the table appropriately, sitting among others, drinking milk and eating his apple carefully to the core. On finishing eating and drinking, he followed the usual routine of depositing his cup and bowl in the sink, without the need for prompting. Harry sought no interaction with others as they ate and drank, gazing around the room instead. He made fleeting eye contact with an adult when she wished to gain his attention and requested him to, 'Look at me!'

When playing outside, Harry chose to walk along a plank with a short slide at the end. He required continual direction, and repeated prompts, to keep moving along the plank and down the slide. Although he waited his turn, no interaction was sought with peers and Harry spent considerable time gazing around.

Harry's assessment profile (see below) was unremarkable with scores well within the average range for his age; this is despite the relative discrepancy between understanding receptive vocabulary (demonstrated by scored outcome with ***British Picture Vocabulary Scale***) and non-verbal score (demonstrated by scored outcome with ***Raven's Coloured Progressive Matrices***).

Chronological Age:	4.07	Test Age	Centile
British Picture Vocabulary Scale – 3rd Edition (Understanding vocabulary)		<3.09	22
Raven's Coloured Progressive Matrices (Aspects of non-verbal ability)		–	63

One-to-one work required perseverance and clear, literal instructions. Harry demonstrated determined reluctance to hold my hand as we walked to and from Nursery. He made no eye contact, beyond giving a fleeting glance when I said goodbye.

During the **British Picture Vocabulary Scale** assessment, where Harry was required to choose one picture to match a given word from a set of four pictures, he struggled to remain focused and rocked back and forth quite vigorously on his seat. He was very distracted by the range of pictures, often commenting on them. For example, on seeing a sock he said, 'Smelly sock' and on seeing a pencil said, 'Pencil – that's writing.' Sometimes he named all four pictures accurately before making a choice – 'Grey, red, green, blue' and 'Tortoise, fish, crocodile, frog.' On sight of a thumb he said 'Good' making the link with the *thumbs up* sign. Harry also made links between items and their uses, so on seeing a bag he said 'Going out,' and on seeing headphones he said 'Music'. His outcome score fell within the low average range at *centile twenty-two*.

In contrast, focus was much better during the non-verbal assessment (**Raven's Coloured Progressive Matrices**) and the score achieved was well within the high average range for age at *centile sixty-three*. At times, Harry backed up his thoughts with words that demonstrated his measured thinking, for example, 'It's too flat.'

Harry presented with cognitive functioning within the expected range for his age, alongside typically specific difficulties associated with his Autism Spectrum Disorder diagnosis.

Joe (English is home and sole language)

We met when Joe was nine years, seven months. He is an example of a child with a range of traits that could potentially attract multiple labels beyond those he had received by the age of six. By now, in Year Five, the wide extent of his needs was becoming increasingly evident. Slow speech development and being late to reach motor milestones had led to diagnoses of Verbal Dyspraxia and Developmental Co-ordination Disorder (DCD) by the age of six. Increasingly, Joe presented with issues relating to the social use and understanding of language which were impacting on his interaction and relationships with others; an Autism Spectrum Disorder had not been diagnosed.

Joe's standardised assessment outcomes (see below) demonstrated marked strengths with mechanical reading and spelling accuracy in particular. Weak short-term auditory memory (demonstrated by scored outcome with *Digit Repetition Test of Short-term Auditory Memory*) is noteworthy and weak performance on drawing a person reflects his earlier DCD diagnosis. Other scores are unremarkable, falling comfortably within the average range for his age.

Chronological Age:	9.07		Test Age	Centile
British Picture Vocabulary Scale – 3rd Edition (Understanding Vocabulary)			10.0	55
Raven's Coloured Progressive Matrices (Non-verbal)			–	25
Short Term Auditory Memory: Digit Repetition			–	10
Goodenough Draw-a-Person			6.03	–
Single Word Reading Test (nfer Form 2)			14.06	91
Vernon Spelling Test – 3rd Edition			11.01	75
Text Reading: Neale Analysis of Reading Ability (Form 1)	Accuracy		11.04	72
	Comprehension		9.04	45

Class Teacher described Joe as *socially sensitive*, finding ignoring provocations from peers challenging, and this impacted on his speed in settling to tasks. Joe's tendency to ignore learning objectives and go off at tangents was also highlighted, along with his finding transitions tricky. Joe's tracked academic progress was reported to be broadly within the expected range for his age, with slow speed of working and, therefore, limited output identified as the most significant hindrance to higher achievement.

Joe engaged with me immediately, during one-to-one work, making and maintaining appropriate eye contact and gesticulating frequently as he spoke. His demeanour remained quite serious throughout. Some word-finding issues were evident from the outset and Joe benefited from suggested optional responses at times. In conversation he had a tendency to give too much detail, demonstrating a lack of awareness of when he should stop. At times, I had to be quite firm, cutting conversations short, in order to get through the necessary tasks. Speech was also quite precise and specific and, on a number of occasions, Joe preceded something he wanted to say by my name, as though to ensure having gained my attention first, 'Mrs Spence, I will see you after break.' Sometimes he made random comments, entirely unrelated to conversation topics or tasks, such as, 'Mrs Spence, I had cold *Weetabix* this morning.'

Joe shared his irritation at some children's comments, 'Some people at my class say I work at Costa!'; this jibe was linked to his surname. He seemed distracted by his own thoughts at times, which impacted on focus. He became overly concerned regarding the possibility of missing break time, checking his watch at regular intervals, despite having been reassured at the start that he would not miss out. Joe mentioned going on holiday to Norfolk soon. When I showed interest in his dog, he suggested I could come to Norfolk too.

Joe remembered to return after play time, bringing his maths workbook with him. I had not asked to see his workbook, but he was keen to share the contents; when asked about the gaps (incomplete pages) he explained that he had run out of time. Joe was also keen to share his *Target Book* which had three targets: *I will start my task straight away, I won't argue with other children, and I will show good manners.* Joe clearly found the book useful and helpful for self-monitoring, explaining how the system worked.

Joe rated his enjoyment of school very highly, allocating a score of 5/5 and telling me, 'I absolutely like it!' When asked directly, he was unable to identify the most and least enjoyable aspects of school but, as time elapsed, he shared a few grievances, explaining that he felt some people were 'mean' to him at times. Joe clearly found some comments irritating and gave examples 'You're a baby!' and 'You're in love with . . . !' He confided, 'Sometimes I get angry and sometimes not. If I get wound up I ask if I can go to another class to do my work.' Joe identified 'listening, handwriting (joining my letters) and typing' as personal strengths at school, identifying 'football' as an area he finds more challenging. He named three special friends, two girls and a boy.

Joe's life beyond school seemed very active with participation in multiple pursuits. He mentioned developing his touch-typing skills, using *Dance Mat Touch-typing* and playing football at another local school. When asked if he belonged to a football club, Joe explained, 'It's *special football*, cos I'm Dyspraxic.' He spoke of learning to play several musical instruments: piano, baritone horn, guitar and drums.

His **British Picture Vocabulary Scale** score, at *centile fifty-five* and *age equivalent ten years*, fell just within the *high average range* for age. In contrast, his **Short-term Auditory Memory** score fell to *centile ten* and was within the *moderately below average* range for chronological age. This means that, despite good understanding of vocabulary, Joe would struggle to retain verbal information and instructions long enough to act on them.

Joe's standardised spelling score outcome fell within the *high average range* at *centile seventy-five* and *age equivalent eleven years, one month*. His single word reading score was particularly high at *centile ninety-one* and *age equivalent fourteen years, six months*. The text reading *accuracy* score was also good at *centile seventy-two* and *age equivalent eleven years, four months.* Use of appropriate expression when reading aloud was minimal and gave the sense that Joe was not reading with complete understanding. Despite this, his reading *comprehension* score at *centile forty-five* and *age equivalent nine years, four months*, was almost age appropriate. Joe *never* chose to re-refer to the text when unsure of responses to questions.

Joe's writing and drawing of a person reflected issues relating to his earlier diagnosis of Developmental Co-ordination Disorder. Using his right hand and applying a suitable grip, Joe pressed excessively as though seeking sensory feedback, holding the pen/pencil very tightly. He made consistent use of his left hand to stabilise paper, sometimes resting his head on this arm. When drawing, Joe appeared to be using his *whole arm*, as opposed to fine finger movements; this impacted significantly on pencil control. Lack of detail and sense of proportion and weak fine motor control resulted in the low outcome score at *age equivalent six years, three months.* Joe would have included even less detail had I not provided prompts, such as 'Anything else your person needs?' Following these, Joe added more detail: ears, arms and fingers.

Unlike when drawing, Joe wrote using fine finger, rather than whole arm movements, perhaps reflecting greater practice time devoted to handwriting. He had developed a large yet even cursive script of well-formed and joined letters. Letters were well positioned on lines and adequate spaces left between words. Despite this, writing is clearly hard work for Joe and he welcomed breaks intermittently and opportunities to shake his hands. When asked to write a short paragraph about himself or somebody he knows well, Joe displayed considerable reluctance, commenting, 'Damn it!' Realising that he had over-stepped the mark when reminded of his third target – 'I will show good manners' – Joe responded with a wry smile and agreed, by way of my suggested compromise, to write just two sentences about himself. Prior to this, he had asked if he could get his laptop as his hand was getting tired. Both sentences made sense with correct punctuation and accurate spelling in context.

Approaches to supporting children like Harry and Joe, who experience challenges with social communication – activities and strategies that experience has shown can make a positive difference

It is important to emphasise again that what follows are not magic wands and the impact of any strategy, activity or programme will depend heavily on the rigour with which they are implemented/delivered. Remember too that all children are unique and there are no hard and fast rules or foolproof strategies; sometimes, it is a case of trial and error and maximising use of those that work for an individual child.

Activities to help develop targeted skills and accelerate progress

Commercially produced programmes can be helpful in as much as they can provide examples and templates which can be replicated and personalised according to individual need. Although personalising a programme is always best, this can be very time consuming and therefore is not always practical; this is when picking and choosing the most relevant elements of a devised programme can prove useful.

1. Commercially produced programmes that are recommended for consideration include:

    i. ***Talkabout: A Social Communication Skills Package*** which is most appropriate for use with children at Key Stage Two (Years Three – Six), focusing on developing social and friendship skills.

    ii. ***Time to Talk: A Programme to Develop Oral and Social Interaction Skills*** which features a puppet (Ginger Bear) is aimed at children of Reception age and through Key Stage One (Years One and Two).

2. ***Social Stories*** are perhaps the single most effective activity with children of primary school age (see Appendix VI).

3. Sometimes, it can be useful in whole class situations to focus on issues with which some individuals may struggle, but without focusing solely on them. Talking in general terms about how others feel when someone uses a very loud voice in class, for example, and what they might feel like doing in response, can help with understanding potential impact. Discussions and role play, to clarify when it is okay to use a loud voice and when we need to speak quietly, can be helpful and supportive, as can considerations regarding when it is best to whisper or remain silent. Use of puppets with younger children can prove particularly effective.

4. Consider the possibility of setting up a lunchtime group, catering for the more socially vulnerable, but including peer volunteers to model social communication within a supportive and comfortable environment. Allow children to have their lunch here and give the group an appealing name. Provide board games to play after eating and other creative, relaxing activities, such as Origami or colouring, that can be undertaken whilst still chatting.

5. *Given that twin diagnoses of ASD and ADHD (Attention Deficit Hyperactivity Disorder) are sometimes made, activities listed in Section Three, for developing the skills of children with ADHD, may also be helpful to others in this group.*

Strategies to enhance accessibility and inclusion in the classroom and beyond

1. Provide visual timetables at school (whole class or individual) as an alternative, augmentative means of communication; make use of visual timetables beyond school too. *As necessary, each morning, use a visual timetable* to prepare the child for the day ahead including, where possible, any changes in routine. As activities are completed they can be crossed off or removed, reinforcing the need to move on to the next activity. Accompany this with clear and simple verbal directives: 'Game/writing/play time *is finished*! *Next,* it is story!' A *home version of a visual timetable* might be useful preparation for non-school days.

2. Display a chart on the classroom door/in the cloakroom with a visual checklist of what needs to be taken home. Try such charts at home to remember what needs to be taken to school.

3. Maximise use of other visual support to aid understanding. Use objects and calendars, for example, to help understanding of sequence and predict what is likely to happen. Try use of a *First* and *Next* chart with activity pictures to prepare for future activities/tasks in the sequence they will be undertaken.

4. When engaged in activities that require turn-taking, provide an object to hold as a visual indication of whose turn it is.

5. Make use of visual cues as prompts, such as a picture of an ear to prompt the need for careful listening or a hand signal to prompt the need to speak more quietly.

6. Give warnings prior to *task changes and short-term transitions* – 'We will be finishing in two minutes.' or 'We will be leaving when the taxi arrives.'

7. Where possible, give warnings prior to *routine changes* at school and beyond: for example, details of who will be supporting/supply teachers.

8. Where possible, *prepare for special events and routine changes* (watch the hall being set up for theatre groups, restarting school again after holiday, visits, non-uniform school days etc). Use photographs of people and places involved. This will help children to feel more secure and confident in dealing with whatever lies ahead.

9. Ensure careful preparation for major transitions, such as when moving up into the next year group at school. Consider additional visits to the new classroom and a one-to-one meeting with the new class teacher, backed up with photographs of the new classroom with the child in it and of the child with the new teacher. Photographs can be viewed regularly over the holiday period as reassurance and preparation for what lies ahead. This procedure can be useful for helping to smooth other major transitions, such as moving house.

10. *Scaffold abstract instructions* to clarify meaning – for example, 'It is snack time. This means go to collect your fruit/biscuit/sandwich and bring it to the table to eat.'

11. Clarify expectations simply in a specific and direct way, *explaining what you want* so that there is no doubt – 'Joe, sit still!' 'Joe, good listening!' *Keep language simple and unambiguous with limited words.* Do away with niceties (for example, use of words such as *please*) and whole sentence instructions or questions, particularly when conformity is required. Instead of 'Joe! Please do not run around my classroom!' try 'Joe! Walk!' Make any reprimands very clear, simple and specific. Instead of 'That's not nice!' try 'Joe! No kicking!'

12. *Where possible, explain what you want* rather than what you don't want. 'Joe! Sit still!' instead of 'Joe, don't move!'

13. *Repeat rather than re-phrase* instructions.

14. Make *ad hoc* use, *as needs arise*, of comic representations (simple stick people with thought and speech bubbles) to teach social conventions, such as sometimes it is okay to *think* something, but *not* to *say* it. If you dislike a person's new hairstyle, for example, you might *think* 'That haircut is awful!' but avoid saying this so as not to hurt the other person's feelings. This idea stems from **Comic Strip Conversations** (see Appendix VII).

15. Consider provision of a classroom-based pop-up tent as a safe, confined space to head for if feeling overwhelmed.

16. It is sometimes helpful to assign *buddy role models* to support inclusion at break times. Having a rota of buddies would minimise over reliance on one person. Select buddies, preferably from volunteers, and give guidance on use of supportive strategies and language.

17. Organised games during *some* break times can help support participation of those less socially confident. This should *not* be an option at every break time as children need the freedom to practise their developing skills more independently.

18. *Again, given that twin diagnoses of ASD and ADHD are sometimes made, strategies listed in Section Three, to enhance accessibility and inclusion among those with ADHD, may also be helpful to others in this group.*

Section 3

Social, Emotional and Mental Health

Some children with needs falling into this category have medical diagnoses and others do not. It can be particularly helpful, therefore, when considering social, emotional and mental health issues, to emphasise the *spectrum of needs*, ranging from mild and/or temporary, through to severe and/or long-term. Cognitive profiles of children can vary considerably, from high average and above, to low average and below. That said, weakness with using and understanding language, and its corresponding scope for misunderstanding, is not an uncommon feature.

In recent years, there has been increased emphasis on *mental health* across society. This is reflected in a change to the descriptive wording, used within the updated Code of Practice (2015) when *Social, Emotional and Behaviour Difficulties* became *Social, Emotional and Mental Health (SEMH)*. The revised wording serves to emphasise that mental health needs may be demonstrated via various behaviours, from disruptive or disturbing to withdrawn or isolated. It also reflects a recent move by charities such as *Mind* to de-stigmatise and highlight the prevalence of mental-health issues.

Perhaps care needs to be taken, however, in distinguishing between long-term and severe conditions and a trend towards medical labels for relatively *normal* feelings and mild eccentricities, such as feeling *blue* temporarily, because of circumstance, or a minor, yet manageable, need to undertake certain rituals. Over, and sometimes inappropriate, use of medical labels can be unhelpful, trivialising the needs of those with the most severe conditions and inflating the needs of others whose feelings and behaviours are more *normal* and, most importantly, manageable. Helping all children to develop resilience and ability to manage their emotions is the aim, but is particularly pertinent to those more vulnerable for one reason or another.

The school environment has expectations regarding behaviours and conformity. Sometimes, behaviours that have not caused concern before children reach school age can become more apparent when new environmental boundaries and routines are introduced. The extent to which a child has experienced specific preparation before starting school is significant. Expectations of parents or carers, and the early boundaries and routines they have implemented, will impact on children's behaviours and their social, emotional and mental well-being. The style of nurture will also impact on children's readiness for school, making the transition either smoother or more challenging. Many pre-school children will, of course, have participated in full or part-time day care, where the staff manage routines and set boundaries; the quality of such provision is of obvious importance.

A further effect of nurturing style is its potential impact on children's natural tendencies, either exaggerating or minimising personal traits. A highly active child, for example, can benefit greatly from having their energies channelled positively, such as through opportunities for physical pursuits; left to their own devices, and without such intervention, a highly energetic child might exhibit less acceptable, even unruly, behaviours.

Becoming a parent is a life change for which there is no manual or mandatory training. The only *direction* stems from parents' own childhood experiences of *being parented*. Adults who experienced firm boundaries, routines and appropriate affection as children are likely to replicate this in their own approach to parenting; others will not instinctively know to do so.

The importance in early childhood of secure attachments to primary carers is well known. Early neglect, other abuse, sudden separation from carers, lack of continuity of carer, or lack of carer responsiveness and interaction, can impact on children's longer-term social, emotional and mental health. Judgements regarding favourable nurture will vary, but most children in mainstream primary schools present as though having received and continuing to receive appropriate care. Standards will vary and, whilst they might not match your own, they may be adequate.

Many teachers and support staff working with children in schools, myself included, will have had vulnerable children expressing a wish that we were their parents. 'I wish you were my Mum/ Dad!' is not an uncommon sentiment expressed. This can be disconcerting to hear for the first time, when newly qualified, inexperienced and possibly not a parent. A relatively inexperienced, yet highly competent, Teacher was quite perplexed when a child mentioned her wish that she was her Mother and the Head Teacher her Father. In a simple and innocent way this child had recognised her Teacher's and Head Teacher's drive and devotion to providing opportunities to learn and develop in a safe, caring and emotionally warm environment.

This Section suggests guidance on two distinct groups within the scope of SEMH. First, there is presentation of children with a diagnosis of Attention Deficit Hyperactivity Disorder (ADHD), and then of children with undiagnosed, high incidence SEMH.

Attention Deficit Hyperactivity Disorder – insight

Some identified with SEMH needs may have medically diagnosed disorders such as Attention Deficit Hyperactivity Disorder (ADHD). This is a collection of behavioural symptoms including inattentiveness, hyperactivity and impulsiveness. Such symptoms sometimes become more obvious when a child starts school and new expectations and structures are imposed. The condition tends to run in families.

Diagnosis is made by specialists, following referral by a General Practitioner. There is no simple test for ADHD; such a diagnosis often follows observation and completion of questionnaires by schools and parents or carers. Questionnaires usually require opinions on the prevalence and extent of a range of associated behaviours. At times, opinions of schools and parents or carers differ, partly because of variations in children's behaviours within the two contexts of school and home, and partly because views, by their nature, are subjective. Sometimes, even the opinions of medical professionals can vary on whether a diagnosis is appropriate.

Over the years, many more little boys than girls have been referred to me with school concerns associated with ADHD traits. They have also often been very young in their year groups with summer birthdays, suggesting maturity and school readiness may be factors.

Medication is sometimes prescribed to help improve concentration and reduce impulsive tendencies. Some types are to be taken every day and some on school days only. Breaks in the treatment are sometimes recommended to establish if medication is still needed. Use of medication is not always acceptable to parents and carers; some worry about side effects and others are simply uncomfortable using drugs to control behaviours.

Many children demonstrate some ADHD traits without formal diagnosis but, whether diagnosed or not, the same activities and supportive strategies can prove helpful.

Attention Deficit Hyperactivity Disorder case examples (Hassan and Freddie)

Hassan

Hassan presented as a very vulnerable little boy. He had been diagnosed with Attention Deficit Hyperactivity Disorder and prescribed medication to address this. He was new on roll and had joined the school mid-way through Year Three, having attended a local junior school prior to this. We met when he was aged seven years and nine months. School reported that medication was not taken regularly and this had impacted on Hassan's ability to engage and focus consistently in class.

Hassan's assessment profile (see below) highlighted most outcome scores within the average range for his age; this included relative strength in his ability to listen and remember (demonstrated by scored outcome with *Digit Repetition Short Term Auditory Memory* exercise). Weak understanding of receptive vocabulary (demonstrated by scored outcome with *British Picture Vocabulary Scale*) stood out and contrasted with good reading *accuracy* scores (demonstrated by scored outcomes with *Neale Analysis of Reading Ability* and *NFER Single Word Reading Test*). Reading *comprehension* score was also good, relative to understanding of receptive vocabulary (demonstrated by scored outcome with *Neale Analysis of Reading Ability*).

Chronological Age:		7.09	Test Age	Centile
British Picture Vocabulary Scale – 3rd Edition (Understanding Vocabulary)			5.05	9
Single Word Reading: NFER – Graded Word Reading Test (Form 1)			7.09	48
Text Reading: Neale Analysis of ReadingAbility (Form 1)	Accuracy		8.0	52
	Comprehension		7.01	26
Vernon Spelling Test – 3rd Edition			–	19
Short Term Auditory Memory: Digit Repetition			–	47
Goodenough Draw a Person Test (Aston Index)			7.0	–
Raven's Coloured Matrices (Non-verbal)			–	16

Observation took place in class, over a thirty minute period during an afternoon session, when a new topic on World War Two was introduced via discussion and film clips. Hassan's engagement and participation were minimal and he appeared to be in a world of his own for much of the time. He pulled and clicked his fingers or rubbed his lips intermittently, rarely looked at the speakers (Class Teacher or peers) and stared into space for sustained periods. There were fleeting moments when he appeared to make an effort to engage, almost as though he had just remembered that he needed to do so, but engagement was short-lived and his responses to collective instructions were consistently delayed. During paired and individual work, Hassan required one-to-one instructions or prompts, to get started and, even then, instructions were either inadequately or inaccurately followed.

Hassan had arrived late at school on the morning scheduled for our one-to-one work, explaining that he was sometimes late 'Because my brother takes long to get dressed.' Before leaving the classroom for one-to-one work, Hassan confirmed with Class Teacher that he had not taken his medication that morning, commenting, 'My Mum said she needs to buy more.' (A reward chart had been set up in school with stickers awarded on days when medication had been taken.) When asked subsequently if taking medication helped him at school, he agreed, 'Helps me to read properly and not mess about.'

In contrast to weak engagement in class, Hassan engaged quite well on a one- to-one basis in a distraction-free environment, making and maintaining reasonable eye contact, responding appropriately in conversation and cooperating with the range of tasks presented. He seemed tired, yawning and rubbing his eyes intermittently. According to Hassan, he had gone to bed at eleven o' clock the night before and did so every night, 'After my Mum picks my Dad up from work.' Hassan pulled and clicked his finger joints continually, at regular intermissions. He was receptive to sticker rewards for task completion and very keen to show others his football stickers on his way outside at play time.

According to Hassan, he left his previous school because of bullying, 'Some people bullying me. Every time I ask them if I can play they say no! People were making me cry. They pushed and kicked me and said I'm stupid.' When asked if he thought his teacher would say that he is good at listening in class, Hassan recognised that this would not be the case, 'I'm being silly – making faces at Megan.' When asked why he does this, Hassan commented, 'Want her to laugh. Want her to play with me – be my friend.' Beyond school, Hassan reported spending his time using a computer, either listening to music or playing games with his brother; his favourite game was called *Bomb it*.

The outcome of the receptive vocabulary assessment (understanding) with the ***British Picture Vocabulary Scale***, at centile nine and age equivalent five years, five months, highlighted below average understanding which would impact on comprehending instructions and information in class. In contrast, his ***Digit Repetition Short Term Auditory Memory*** outcome score fell within the mid average range at centile forty-seven. This demonstrated ability to listen and remember in a distraction-free environment and suggested potential ability to do so within the classroom, particularly with the support of medication. *Retaining information, however, is all very well, but of limited use if understanding is sketchy.*

Both text reading and single word reading *accuracy* scores were age appropriate and within the mid average range at centiles fifty-two and forty-eight and age equivalents eight and seven years, nine months respectively. As expected, given weak receptive vocabulary, text reading comprehension was weaker, but his score still fell within the low average range at centile twenty-six and age equivalent seven years, one month. *This suggested that Hassan had been effectively taught strategies to answer reading comprehension questions correctly, despite weak real understanding.* Limitations with comprehension were evident from minimal self-correction of reading accuracy from context, limited observation of full stops and restricted use of expression.

When writing, Hassan used his right hand and made use of his left to stabilise paper. He was able to write his first and surname accurately; the only error involved reversal of the letter *y*. When asked to write two or three sentences about something he loves doing, Hassan had no hesitation regarding the subject choice (football); he began writing straightaway and without reluctance. He produced one long sentence, which made sense. Handwriting was very large, yet clear, and a combination of print and cursive script, with letters inconsistently positioned on lines and inadequate spaces left between words. Hassan made appropriate use of a full stop and whilst most spelling in context was accurate, vocabulary use was limited with overuse of certain words, again reflecting his area of particular weakness.

Freddie

Freddie also presented as a very vulnerable boy. He had been diagnosed with both Attention Deficit Hyperactivity Disorder and Autism Spectrum Disorder and joined the school in Year Two, having attended another local primary school prior to this. We met when he was eight years, four months and in Year Four. Freddie had been prescribed medication to address his ADHD symptoms, but school reported inconsistency with taking this at home, sometimes because of his refusal to co-operate. School also mentioned that Freddie sometimes arrived at school not having had breakfast and always seemed tired. Freddie's inclination to gravitate very closely to support staff had been observed, as had his interest in their

personal possessions, such as watches or jewellery. At the time of our meeting, Freddie's class was shared by *three* Class Teachers and he was supported by a range of Teaching Assistants, timetabled over the course of a week.

Freddie's assessment profile (see below) highlighted marked weakness with listening, reflective of his ADHD diagnosis (demonstrated by scored outcome with the *Short Term Auditory Memory Digit Repetition* exercise). His understanding of receptive vocabulary (demonstrated by scored outcome with *British Picture Vocabulary Scale*) is a relative strength. Use of standardised reading and spelling assessments was inappropriate because of Freddie's early stage of acquisition of these skills.

Chronological Age:	8.04	Test Age	Centile
British Picture Vocabulary Scale – 3rd Edition (Understanding Vocabulary)		6.06	18
Raven's Coloured progressive Matrices (Non-verbal)		–	9
Short Term Auditory Memory: Digit Repetition		–	2
Goodenough Draw-a-Person (Aston Index)		5.09	–

Brief observation took place in class when children were required to share *Roman facts* with everyone, having collated these in pairs, following computer research. Freddie had no additional support in class at this time and clutched a cuddly toy upon which he focused entirely. His work partner, an apparently able boy, did his best to ignore Freddie's antics, including when he thrust the cuddly toy in his face. Freddie seemed oblivious to Class Teacher's requests even to *look in the right direction* and even when such requests were preceded by his name.

During independent work, Freddie was up and out of his seat much of the time, pushing the cuddly toy down the shirt of a boy sitting opposite, before *walking* the toy along the classroom wall to the window. He engaged with the task fleetingly when supported directly by the Class Teacher. *Observation suggested the toy may have been more of a distraction than a support.* It may have been brought from home to support transition to school, or provided by school to help meet a sensory need, through having something soft and comforting to hold.

Freddie willingly left the classroom to work with me on a one-to-one basis. He made minimal eye contact initially until a conversation about his pets; Freddie became quite animated at this point and told me about his dog, Dipsy, describing her as, 'Just black and a little bit of white. She cuddles me.' He also talked about his cat, Poppet, described by Freddie as 'All colours, 'cept on blue and purple.'

As time elapsed, Freddie initiated and extended further conversation, showing great interest in my watch, with incessant questions. He yawned continually. Being unfamiliar with Freddie's speech, clarity was an issue at times. He rarely sat still, rocking his chair onto two legs, slumping across the table, fiddling with a ring binder and kicking chair legs. Although he admitted to enjoying school, Freddie identified his favourite time of day as 'going home.' At home, he talked of playing alone on his X-Box, explaining, 'Cos we're not online.' Freddie considered, 'Everyone in class' to be his friend.

He was able to read just 7/32 high frequency words from **Phase 2**: (a, mum, the, to, I, no, go) recognising these by sight. Despite having knowledge of all **Phase 2** and **3** letter sounds, apart from *d*, *b* and *q*, he made no attempt to apply phonic strategies to decode *vowel consonant* (at, up etc) or *consonant vowel consonant* words (cup, pit etc).

Freddie demonstrated that he could write his first name, but would not attempt his surname, eventually writing the first letter when I asked if he could do this. Unlike when drawing, Freddie made no use of his left hand to stabilise paper when writing. Although they were poorly formed, he was able to write letters to match most single letter sounds, confusing the orientation of *t* and *j*, writing a capital letter *f* and omitting *v* and *w*. Use of phonic knowledge to encode words for spelling was very limited. Freddie was able to spell *Mum*.

Freddie's drawing of a person was very immature for his age in terms of the level of detail included and poorly developed motor control; his outcome score, at five years, nine months, was well below that expected for a child of his chronological age. He drew with his right hand and made use of his left to stabilise paper, but held the pencil about half way up its shaft, applying a loose grip which reduced control.

The outcome of the receptive vocabulary assessment (understanding) with the **British Picture Vocabulary Scale** *was more promising and he achieved a score* just within the low average range for age at centile eighteen and age equivalent six years, six months. Freddie managed to sit still and maintain focus during this task, supported by its use of pictures. *I had undertaken this assessment with Freddie previously, when he was in Year Two and aged six years, ten months. At that time, he achieved a score within the moderately below average range for age at centile five and age equivalent four years, eleven months. Updated score demonstrated good progress.* In contrast, Freddie's approach to the non-verbal assessment (**Raven's Coloured Matrices**) was less measured. He worked very quickly, often making impulsive choices; hence the outcome score achieved, at centile nine, may be a less reliable indicator of ability.

Approaches to Supporting Children, like Hassan and Freddie, who experience traits associated with Attention Deficit Hyperactivity Disorder – activities and strategies that experience has shown can make a positive difference

It is important to emphasise again that what follows are not magic wands and the impact of any strategy, activity or programme will depend heavily on the rigour with which they are implemented/delivered. Remember, too, that all children are unique and there are no hard and fast rules or foolproof strategies; sometimes, it is a case of trial and error and maximising use of those that work for an individual child.

Activities to help develop targeted skills and accelerate progress

Many activities can be undertaken on an *ad hoc* or incidental basis at school or beyond.

1. Refer to *lifestyle* advice for parents and carers at Appendix VIII: *Developing children's attention skills.*

2. Try physical activities to promote calmness and better regulate overall alertness. It may be helpful to spend a few minutes doing activities at crucial times of day (first thing in the morning, after lunch and after break time). Activities to consider include the following: running around the playground, climbing on outdoor equipment, such as monkey bars, marching or jumping on the spot, helping to move things around the school or running errands.

3. Try playing simple eye contact games in class where children *pass* eye contact on from one to another and everyone must be ready to *receive* eye contact at any time throughout the game.

4. *Listening to Silence* Increase children's awareness of sound and silence. Sit quietly together for a minute and then take turns to whisper anything heard, such as clock ticking, person breathing, door slamming etc. Try the same activity outside.

5. *Copy the Rhythm* Use a drum to bang or maracas to shake a set number of times. Having listened, can children repeat what they have heard?

6. *On Your Marks, Get Set, Go!* Ask children to colour a square (on squared paper) or colour a given section of a picture on hearing the word *Go!* Vary the time lapses between saying it.

7. *Jumping Bean* Ask children to crouch down. When you clap your hands or bang a drum they must jump up.

8. *Simon Says* Give instructions for children to perform. Start off with one and then build up to two – *Simon says put hands in the air.* (One instruction) *Simon says put hands in the air and stamp your feet.* (Two instructions)

9. *Mimic the Action* Children work in pairs standing or sitting opposite each other and take turns to be the *Leader* or *Follower*. *Leaders* are given actions to mime, such as waving or climbing. The *Follower* mimics the actions of the *Leader*.

10. *I Went on Holiday* Take turns to add items that you would pack. Take turns to say, *I went on holiday and I packed* _____. Each time you must remember all of the items packed previously. Can you get as far as remembering six items or even more?

11. *Help children to make simple puppets* of the main character(s) in a story; as they listen to the story they can hold up the puppet(s) each time a character's name is heard.

12. *Given that twin diagnoses of ADHD and ASD are sometimes made, activities listed in Section Two, for developing the skills of children with ASD, may also be helpful to others in this group.*

Strategies to enhance accessibility and inclusion in the classroom and beyond

1. Medication can be useful for helping to temper, control and manage impetuous, impulsive behaviours, enabling satisfactory engagement with learning and increasing capacity for making progress.

2. If parents or carers have decided to accept prescribed medication for their child, as with other medicines it is important that this is administered as prescribed. In my experience, parents often manage medication, without direct involvement from school, but where life beyond school is less organised or a child demonstrates reluctance to cooperate, school might support the process. Medication could be administered by the parent or carer on arrival at school, in the presence of support staff, for example. Provision of an edible reward, such as fruit, often encourages cooperation.

3. Refer to advice for parents and carers at Appendix IX: *Promote better behaviour choices*.

4. In recent years, there have been moves to vary the personnel involved with targeted support, to reduce children's dependence on and attachment to particular individuals, allowing for working with a range of adults with different personality traits, styles and expectations. This is not always in a child's best interests; where life beyond school is turbulent there is increased need for *consistency* and *security* at school. Sometimes, if there is a bereavement or a parent is hospitalised, for example, such a need might be temporary.

5. Encourage *self-help strategies* i.e. make children aware of methods that help them to engage and maintain attention: *watch* the speaker; *minimize* distractions by choosing a place to sit, for example, without window view/noise from corridor/away from others they may find distracting.

6. *Precede instructions to the class or group with Give me Five* to gain everyone's attention and help focus *(Eyes looking, Ears listening, Lips closed, Hands still, Brains ready).*

7. Support instructions and other information given verbally with visual back up, including actions, to support focus.

8. Where possible and necessary, minimise visual distractions by providing a low stimulation, quieter work space. Consider a simple work station, facing a wall, with cardboard screens perhaps. (Remember that although plentiful visual stimuli can be helpful to many, they can be distracting and unhelpful to some.)

9. Bear in mind that visual back-up, such as sand-timers, can prove more distracting than helpful.

10. Use of ear defenders can help reduce auditory distractions.

11. Sometimes, allowing manipulation of a small piece of Blu tack meets a sensory need, assisting focus and ability to sit still. Alternatively, consider providing stress balls to squeeze or purpose-made fiddle toys; to minimise misuse of these, rules regarding use need to be crystal clear. Monitor use of these to establish whether children find them helpful rather than a further distraction!

12. Sometimes, provision of a carpet tile helps to mark out visually the boundaries of an individual's sitting space on the floor; this can help support remaining seated within a contained space.

13. *Rest breaks* might also be incorporated within lessons so children have opportunities to get up and move around. Sometimes, additional provision needs to be put in place to enable participation in the Key Stage One and Two National Curriculum Tests, taken in Years Two and Six respectively. These are known as **Access Arrangements**, where adjustments such as prompts and rest breaks can be made to support attention and concentration. Such **Access Arrangements** should be *based on normal classroom practice*, where children routinely benefit from movement breaks and prompts (visual and/or sensory cues) to help maintain focus in lessons.

14. *Again, given that twin diagnoses of ADHD and ASD are sometimes made, strategies listed in Section Two, for developing the skills of children with ASD, may also be helpful to others in this group.*

Undiagnosed, high-incidence Social, Emotional and Mental Health needs – insight

Children can sometimes find unrealistic expectations of their performance stressful; such expectations might be held by school and/or home. Schools, under pressure to hit targets, exemplified by relentless rounds of testing and assessment, may inadvertently pass the feeling of pressure on to children. Those able enough and adequately resilient can manage such pressures. Others, particularly those who experience barriers to learning, such as a Specific Language Impairment (see Section Two) combined with having English as an additional language, find this more challenging, with potential for negative impacts on self-esteem.

As parents and carers, most of us are keen that our children are successful. Sometimes, aspirations can be overly ambitious which may lead to a sense of never performing well enough, a fear of making mistakes and extreme perfectionism.

Most young children thrive when parents or carers engage and interact with them on a regular basis; these opportunities often provide access to positive social and emotional role models, enabling incidental learning. This requires time allocation, sometimes from busy schedules, and a willingness to prioritise. Unfortunately, sometimes there seems reluctance to ever prioritise children's over parent/carers' own needs, with children having to *fit in* continually. This can result in a lack of balanced activities offered beyond school and, sometimes, over-reliance on technology as a means of *babysitting*, keeping children quiet and occupied.

Undiagnosed, high-incidence Social, Emotional and Mental Health case examples (Gavin, Jack, Urszula and Amelia)

Gavin

Gavin had joined a Reception class at the beginning of a new school year. We met when he was aged four years and eleven months, having been at school for almost a term. Generally, he was reported to make minimal eye contact, follow his own agenda and resist persuasion to engage with tasks not of his choosing or of interest to him; in short, if he did not wish to do something, he would refuse. It had been observed that Gavin tended to be more responsive to requests from Class Teacher than to those made by the Teaching Assistant. Class Teacher expressed concerns regarding the future, as Gavin progressed to Year One with its increased structure and less freedom.

Gavin's assessment profile (see below) confirmed cognitive ability within the expected range for his age and particularly good understanding of receptive vocabulary (demonstrated by scored outcome with _British Picture Vocabulary Scale_).

Chronological Age:	4.11	Test Age	Centile
British Picture Vocabulary Scale – 3rd Edition (Understanding Vocabulary)	5.02		72
Raven's Coloured Matrices (Non-verbal)		–	16
Goodenough Draw a Person Test (Aston Index)	4.11		–

Observation took place in class, over a forty-five minute period, during an afternoon session. Children were carpet-based initially for discussion work and direction on the afternoon's planned activities. Latterly, children were free to select from options available and sometimes asked to participate in adult-led tasks.

Gavin was encouraged to sit on his _carpet spot_, which he did, following a direct instruction preceded by his name. When sitting, he appeared to seek continual sensory stimulation, his hand up and inside his shirt or down his trousers. Gavin did not respond to collective class instructions to follow various actions and wandered off the carpet before his group was called to do so.

He collected a cuddly toy from the _story_ corner and took it to the pirate ship role play area. Within this area, a semi-enclosed space had been created beneath a table, boarded up with cardboard on two sides; Gavin headed here. He spent twenty minutes lying on top of the cuddly toy which he had positioned between his legs. Gavin appeared to seek sensory stimulation, rocking continually back and forth on the toy. At one stage, he was asked to come out from under the table by the Teaching Assistant who explained that he might get knocked and hurt. Gavin ignored her request and remained rocking back and forth on the toy. She made a second request, giving Gavin until she counted to three to respond; again, she was ignored. A few minutes later, the Teaching Assistant called Gavin to make a paper fish at the table with other children. Gavin did not respond; it was as though she had not spoken to him.

On occasion, other children initiated interaction with Gavin, crawling under the table next to him, but he was unresponsive, continuing to rub himself against the toy. When I asked if the toy was his favourite, Gavin responded and told me, 'It's a white polar bear. We used to have a big polar bear, but it went missing. Some pirates got it.' Realising that he considered himself a *doggy pirate*, I asked if this *pirate dog* ever came out of his *kennel*. Gavin responded, 'He comes out sometimes, when he's on dry land.' When I told him that I would like to see if he could make a fish, Gavin shot out from under the table and headed for the *story* corner. Here, he resumed his previous position, lying and rocking on top of the polar bear toy, again positioned between his legs. His face remained expressionless.

Gavin responded when the Class Teacher asked, 'Are you alright, Gav? Are you going to do me a flower?' He followed requests accurately to find *m* for mummy, *d* for daddy, *m* for Mrs and *h* for Harry on an alphabet chart. At times, he sought reassurance, 'Is this it?' He accepted help with holding the pencil and responded positively to Class Teacher's attempts to jolly him along in an animated way, giving some eye contact and occasional flickers of smiles.

Gavin left the classroom readily and engaged with me immediately, taking my hand. During one-to-one work he made many spontaneous observations and asked questions relating to things that captured his interest. He noticed that the stair rail was wooden on one side and silver on the other, asking, 'Why is one wooden and one silver?' On seeing a picture of a pumpkin he told me, 'We put a candle in with no real fire. It smelt of rotten eggs.' He noticed a sink in the corner and asked, 'Is that where they wash their hands in class?'

Eye contact made was often minimal, but improved over time, depending on Gavin's level of interest in tasks presented or conversation topics. He responded positively to smiling and exaggerated facial expressions to encourage his sustained engagement when this was waning.

According to Gavin, he felt happiest at school 'When I'm playing outside.' He also enjoyed school lunches and eagerly described the day's menu, 'Meatballs and 'tato, strawberry mousse and vanilla icecream.' Gavin considered a number of children in class to be friends and mentioned his enjoyment of playing games such as *Hide and Seek* together. He admitted to feeling sad at school 'When somebody hurts me. I bumped heads when I was in the playground. Sometimes Mrs. Harry is grumpy with me when I hurt somebody! It makes Mrs Harry's face happy when I'm playing so nicely.'

The outcome of the receptive vocabulary assessment (understanding) with the **British Picture Vocabulary Scale**, at centile seventy-two and age equivalent five years, two months, highlighted understanding within the high average range for his age. He initiated a few additional comments linked to his observations of pictures, drawing my attention to a picture of a beehive and telling me 'That's my skull!' on seeing a picture of one.

Gavin engaged somewhat less well with the non-verbal assessment (**Raven's Coloured Progressive Matrices**) and did not appear to consider all options consistently before giving responses; nevertheless, his outcome score fell just within the low average range at centile sixteen.

Gavin's drawing of a person was age appropriate in terms of the level of detail included, with an outcome score of four years, eleven months. Left to his own devices, he employed a left-handed *fist* pencil grip. Gavin responded to prompts to self-correct, but his grip remained loose and he held the pencil high up its shaft, both of which impacted on control.

When reading, Gavin demonstrated instant recall of all **Phase 2** and **3** letter sounds (see Appendix II), apart from *qu* which he read as the word *up*. He recognised his name and the word *I* and made some good attempts at using known phonics to decode several **Phase 2** words. He was able to read the sounds *a-t*, *a-n*, *i-n*, *i-s*, *d-a-d*, *u-p* and *m-u-m* in sequence, but unable to blend these to give corresponding whole words.

Gavin showed some inclination towards swapping hands when asked if he could write his name; a task he almost managed in huge unwieldy form. Letter formation was hampered by weak pencil grip and control. He struggled to write any letters to match the sounds *s*, *a*, *t*, *p*, *i*, *n*, achieving greater success when asked to find letters before writing them.

Gavin's case is an example of a little boy with age appropriate cognitive ability, displaying unusual behaviours in class, including resistance to some demands and a need for repetitive sensory stimulation. The cause of such behaviours may be due to anxiety within a busy classroom environment as they were not apparent on a one-to-one basis, within a quiet workspace.

Jack

Jack had joined a Reception class at the beginning of a new school year. We met when he was aged four years and eleven months. He was described as a lovely little boy, but there were concerns regarding aspects of social and emotional skills and particularly with his perception of fairness. Mother had expressed concerns regarding Jack's willingness to share. School reported a good memory for facts and articulate use of language.

Jack's assessment profile (see below) confirmed good cognitive ability: all outcome scores within the high average range for his age.

Chronological Age:	4.11	Test Age	Centile
British Picture Vocabulary Scale – 3rd Edition (Understanding Vocabulary)		5.02	72
Raven's Coloured Progressive Matrices (Non-verbal)	–		83
Goodenough Draw-a-Person (Aston Index)	6.09		–

Observation took place in class, over a thirty minute period during a morning session. Children were involved with adding two single-digit numbers and number *fans* (sets of cards numbered with digits and tied together) had been distributed to enable all children to participate and respond to all questions on an individual basis. Jack sat at the front on the carpet. He had been allocated a white board and pen instead of a number fan, as had another child.

Jack was very engaged, writing out sums on his board quickly and competently, showing his answers at the appropriate times. At the end of this activity, Jack chose to continue practising writing out sums, which he created independently, on the teacher's white board. He wrote 8+5= and commented, 'Miss Clarke, you can't do this!' He accepted Miss Clarke's *loan* of her fingers so that between them they had enough. Jack arrived at the correct answer and wrote the number 13 accurately and without help.

During one-to-one work Jack was very willing to work with me and well engaged from the outset, cooperating with all tasks presented and maintaining topics of conversation. Occasionally, he initiated conversation and when hearing children playing outside commented, 'I think some children are out playing nicely.'

He worked hard and at a good rate, rising to challenges. Eye contact was minimal initially, but as time elapsed, this increased somewhat. Jack knew that he was four and would be five 'on Christmas.' He remembered my name, having been told just once. Jack counted the steps accurately as we went up the stairs, announcing that there were twenty-two steps altogether. He was pleased to receive stickers for working hard and told me, 'Miss Clarke will be proud of me!'

According to Jack, before starting in a Reception class, he went to 'a baby school' which he described as 'boring.' He highlighted the best thing about school as 'plussing' and recognised this as something he was good at doing. Jack had a best friend with whom he enjoyed playing 'doggy games.' He identified his favourite toy at home as a big dinosaur called Rex.

The outcome of receptive vocabulary assessment (understanding) with the **British Picture Vocabulary Scale**, at centile seventy-two and age equivalent five years, two months, highlighted understanding within the high average range for his age. *When unsure, Jack preferred to say he didn't know rather than have a go.* Similarly, his non-verbal assessment outcome score (**Raven's Coloured Progressive Matrices**) also fell within the high average range at centile eighty-three. Jack made careful, considered choices, yet worked at a good pace, and commented that one pattern looked like a maze. Jack's *drawing of a person* was mature, in terms of the level of detail included and fluency of pencil control; hence his good score at age equivalent six years, nine months. He was keen to ensure the inclusion of five fingers, counting to five as he drew.

When reading, Jack made rigorous use of phonic skills to decode **Phase 2** and **3** words (see Appendix II), achieving considerable success; some he recognised visually, as whole words. There was some confusion between letters *b* and *d*, which is not unusual at this stage. Jack was able to read a few **Phase 4** and **5** words by sight.

When writing, as a left-hander, Jack made effective and consistent use of his right hand to stabilise paper. He applied a suitable pencil grip, but tended to hold the pencil high up the shaft and in a very upright position, rather than resting it on the web between his thumb and index finger.

Jack was very willing to write and took great care with spelling accuracy, demonstrating his ability to spell 25/32 **Phase 2** words correctly. Errors included: *of* (*ov*), *his* (*hiz*) and reversal of the letter *g* when writing the word *big*. Jack became perplexed, and cross with himself, when writing the word *put* as he wrote the letter *b* initially instead of *p*. I rubbed this out, on his request, and he wrote the letter *b* again, becoming annoyed with himself for a second time. Jack persevered and wrote the letter *p* accurately on his third attempt; I sensed that his frustration had potential to escalate if I had not been on hand to rub out errors and play things down. Jack was able to spell a range of *consonant vowel consonant* words (cap, tip etc), making appropriate use of each of the five vowel letters. He was also able to apply knowledge of some **Phase 3** graphemes for accurate spelling, managing ch*i*p, *sh*op, ri*ng*, p*ee*p and c*oin*. As when reading, sometimes Jack confused the letters *b* and *d* and did so when writing his surname. His handwriting was large, but letters were mostly well-formed and consistently lowercase.

Jack was able to write a simple sentence from dictation and to create and write simple sentences of his own. He was aware of the need for 'stops' (full stops), to punctuate sentences, and had awareness of word boundaries, demarcating these with spaces. Much spelling in context was accurate and although he sought help when unsure, asking, 'What comes next?', he was prepared to have a go if encouraged, relying on his phonic knowledge.

Jack's case is an example of a well-motivated and focused little boy with good cognitive ability, making progress at school with acquisition of early literacy and numeracy skills at the expected rate. Not yet five years of age, he was already demonstrating a tendency towards controlling and perfectionist traits, requiring targeted support to help manage these.

Urszula

Urszula had been on roll since Reception. We met when she was in Year Five and aged nine years and eight months. Urszula was described as a quiet girl who seemed very anxious at times, sometimes arriving at school in tears and complaining of feeling unwell. Academic progress had been monitored closely with regular home-school liaison, including via a diary, where Class Teacher had made continual requests for Urszula to read more regularly. School had noted Urszula's apparent anxiety, even when undertaking routine tasks, such as informal reading assessments, with familiar teachers. Reading accuracy was reported to be sound, but comprehension more limited.

Urszula's parents are Polish and, when in Year Four, she had received additional support from the school-based Specialist Teacher for children with English as an Additional Language (EAL). The EAL Teacher had queried Urszula's level of competence with spoken and written Polish; this will, of course, have depended on the extent of exposure to and use of Polish in addition to any direct tuition she may have received. *In my experience, it is not unusual for children to attend schools at weekends for tuition in their home language.*

Urszula's assessment profile (see below) highlighted limited vocabulary and weak short-term auditory memory (demonstrated by scored outcomes with *British Picture Vocabulary Scale* and *Short Term Auditory Memory Digit Repetition* exercise). Both areas of relative weakness would have been impacting on Urszula's ability to keep up with the language of the classroom and comprehend texts read. The discrepancy between reading accuracy and reading comprehension was markedly evident (demonstrated by scored outcomes with *Neale Analysis of Reading Ability*). Detail included in her drawing of a person was age appropriate. Such assessment outcomes suggest the possibility of traits associated with Specific Language Impairment, as described within Section Two. Such hindrances often become more apparent as children move through primary school and the demands of the curriculum increase. These issues may explain Urszula's increased anxiety at school.

Chronological Age:	9.08		Test Age	Centile
British Picture Vocabulary Scale – 3rd Edition (Understanding Vocabulary)	7.06			7
Text Reading: Neale Analysis of Reading Ability (Form 2)	Accuracy	10.10		70
	Comprehension	8.07		28
Goodenough Draw-a-Person (Aston Index)	9.09			–
Short Term Auditory Memory: Digit Repetition	–			13

There was no observation in class, given the nature of concerns and that Urszula was in Year Five, a stage when children often become increasingly self-conscious, keen to fit in socially and minimise differences. During one-to-one work, as time elapsed, she became more relaxed, even initiating some incidental chat. Well-chewed finger nails were evident.

According to Urszula, she had received no formal tuition in Polish, part-time or otherwise. She was born in England and visited Poland for annual holidays. At home, Urszula confirmed speaking English to her two older sisters, but Polish to her parents.

Urszula considered *play time* the most enjoyable element of the school day and identified *art* as her favourite lesson and personal strength. She mentioned her reluctance to participate in class assemblies and admitted that sometimes she did not want to attend school as she felt sick when worried. Urszula spoke of feeling upset sometimes, 'When people call me names – rude names like *idiot*. Friends say it as a joke. Sometimes they don't really like me!' She also confided that she found understanding information and instructions challenging in class, confirming that she asked friends for assistance, 'But they don't always help.'

Urszula referred to her enjoyment of drawing pictures of people in her leisure time. She also spoke of recently taking up horse-riding with a much younger friend.

The outcome of receptive vocabulary assessment (understanding) with the **British Picture Vocabulary Scale** was weak and she achieved a score within the moderately below average range for age *at centile seven and age equivalent seven years, six months.* This confirmed the extent of limitations with comprehending English words. During the task, gaps in Urszula's vocabulary soon became evident; examples included her misunderstanding of the words *rough, solo, pillar, links, adjustable, applauding, inflated, hovering, pedestrian, beaker, parallel and bouquet.* Her outcome score with **Digit Repetition Short-term Auditory Memory** assessment was also weak and within the moderately below average range for age, at *centile thirteen*, despite Urszula's considerable effort and focused approach.

Her *text reading accuracy* score fell within the high average range at centile seventy and age equivalent ten years, ten months. *Text reading comprehension* score was much weaker, but still within the low average range at centile twenty-eight and age equivalent eight years, seven months. *Further probing indicated that Urszula's actual comprehension of what she had read was much weaker than her answers suggested.* Often, she was *unable* to understand key vocabulary in texts and questions; achievement of a standardised score at centile twenty-eight was reflective of effective teaching.

Amelia

Amelia had been on roll since Year Three, having transferred from a local infant to a primary school; at that time, levels of achievement were reported to have been very low. We met when she was in Year Five and aged ten years, two months. By this time, some measurable progress had been observed at school. There were some concerns associated with behaviours and task engagement. Parents, by contrast, believed that Amelia experienced difficulties associated with *dyslexia*, mentioning a family history of the condition.

Amelia's assessment profile (see below) demonstrated very inconsistent outcome scores, ranging from centile one to centile forty-eight; these need to

be regarded with some caution, however, as there were significant issues with task engagement and apparently deliberate errors. One assessment (Short Term Auditory Memory: Digit Repetition) was impossible to complete, such was the extent of Amelia's erratic approach and reluctance.

Chronological Age:		10.02	Test Age	Centile
British Picture Vocabulary Scale – 3rd Edition		5.07		<2
Raven's Coloured Progressive Matrices		–		1
Short Term Auditory Memory: Digit Repetition		–		Unable to complete
Single Word Reading: NFER – Graded Word Reading Test (Form 2)		7.06		8
Text Reading: Neale Analysis of Reading Ability (Form 2)	Accuracy	8.00		18
	Comprehension	7.02		7
	Rate	10.01		48
Vernon Spelling Test – 3rd Edition		–		<2

There was no observation in class, partly because school disagreed with the parents' suggestion regarding *dyslexia* tendencies and requested an objective view of Amelia's performance and approach to tasks on a one-to-one basis.

She was brought out of class and seemed really pleased and quite excited to see me, smiling broadly when we met. She engaged with me very readily, exuding an air of confidence much more advanced than her ten years. Amelia was keen to enquire immediately whether she would remain with me all afternoon and commented, 'I know why you're here!' She declined to elaborate, but continued to grin widely in a way that some might find disconcerting.

Amelia demonstrated significant difficulties sitting still and appropriately. She fidgeted frequently and excessively, often sitting on her leg and slouching right across the table. At other times, she rocked the chair on two legs. I used my phone to time some tasks and Amelia showed huge, almost obsessive interest in the phone rather than the task. She told me, 'I'm really good with i-pads and phones. I go on my Mum's and Dad's phones all the time!' At times, Amelia seemed to struggle with attention and focus. She complained of feeling hungry, at one stage, and soon after, that her neck hurt and then her throat. Task engagement was often very weak, yet Amelia was able to read the time accurately (twenty-five past two) from my analogue, numberless watch, a task with which some children continue to struggle at Year Five and beyond.

Amelia rated her enjoyment of school as 3/5. She would have welcomed increased opportunities to use i-Pads and expressed her dislike of *tests*, especially 'writing tests.' She identified two best friends at school, but never met up with these children during her leisure time. When not at school, according to Amelia, she spent her time watching television and videos or playing games on her tablet. She also mentioned her enjoyment of going shopping and her preference for *Designer* shops as 'I get what I like.' Amelia told me about her ambition to join a Street Dance class.

The outcome of the receptive vocabulary assessment (understanding) with the **British Picture Vocabulary Scale** was very weak and she achieved a score *below centile two and age equivalent five years, seven months.* My impression was that *Amelia seemed to be making errors deliberately so the validity of the outcome score was questionable.* She claimed to be unable to identify pictures to match the following words, for example: *jumping, swimming, fire, thumb* (until I asked her to show me *her own thumbs), tunnel, whistle, nest* and *rectangle.* Similarly, Amelia's approach to the non-verbal assessment (**Raven's Coloured Matrices**) was erratic, with responses impulsive and not at all measured. Her outcome score, at *centile one,* seemed unlikely to be a reliable indicator of ability.

When reading single words, Amelia relied heavily on visual memory, as opposed to application of phonic strategies. Her single word reading assessment outcome score fell within the *moderately below average range for age at centile eight and age equivalent seven years, six months.* Her *text reading* accuracy score was just within the low average range at centile eighteen and age equivalent eight years. *Text reading comprehension was weaker at centile seven and age equivalent seven years, two months.* Re-referral to text, to support answering questions, was observed to be minimal. Interestingly, *reading rate* score, which is often markedly weak in those described as experiencing *dyslexia* traits, was age appropriate at centile forty-eight and age equivalent ten years, one month.

Amelia wrote with her left hand, holding the pencil in a very upright position and pressing very hard as though needing sensory feedback. Her forehead rested on the table as she wrote. She verbalised two sentences about her dog before writing these, 'My dog is called Barbie. Barbie likes her food and we give her meat.' At one point, Amelia told me, 'I can think of really good ideas, but can't write them down!' Handwriting size was inconsistent, with poorly formed letters, and use of punctuation was erratic. Amelia's standardised spelling assessment outcome score was very weak at below centile two.

Overall, Amelia's assessment profile was not typical of a child experiencing *dyslexia*. As described in detail within Section One, children with these traits tend to achieve weaker scores in reading (particularly accuracy and rate) and/or spelling, alongside stronger cognitive or general ability scores (such as scores achieved in the **British Picture Vocabulary Scale** and/or **Raven's Coloured Progressive Matrices**).

Assessment outcomes achieved suggest relatively weak cognitive (general) ability, exacerbated by considerable issues associated with very weak attention, focus and ability to maintain sustained task engagement. This was very evident, even when working on a one-to-one basis, and will have impacted on outcomes. Amelia's apparently deliberate errors suggest the possibility that she may have been attempting to manipulate outcomes to prove having *dyslexia* traits; this is very difficult to achieve without insight into the need to perform well in certain assessments and less well in others.

Amelia's case provides an example of parents looking for a possible label, which they find acceptable in terms of potential stigma, to explain slow progress at school. Acquisition of such a label also distances parents or carers from any behavioural issues which may have arisen as a possible consequence of parenting style.

Approaches to Supporting Children, like Gavin, Jack, Urszula and Amelia who demonstrate high incidence Social, Emotional and Mental Health needs – activities and strategies that experience has shown can make a positive difference

It is important to emphasise again that what follows are not magic wands and the impact of any strategy, activity or programme will depend heavily on the rigour with which they are implemented/delivered. Remember, too, that all children are unique and there are no hard and fast rules or foolproof strategies; sometimes, it is a case of trial and error and maximising use of those that work for an individual child.

Activities to help address management of targeted areas and accelerate progress

1. Where there are concerns regarding children's social, emotional and mental health, it is particularly helpful if written advice from education and/or health professionals involved is shared; this will facilitate a joined-up approach with the needs of the *whole child* highlighted and addressed. Sometimes, parents or carers are best placed to ensure this happens.

2. Referral to *Child and Adolescent Mental Health Services (CAMHS)* may prove helpful, but there are usually long waiting lists; outcomes are unlikely to be *magic wand* solutions so there is a need for *expectation management* and implementation of self-help, home and school-based strategies in the meantime.

3. One-to-one *Mentoring programmes* for vulnerable children within Key Stage Two (Years Three to Six), can provide powerful and effective support where adult mentors become the '*rocks*' in children's lives, *championing* their needs (see Appendix X).

4. *Nurturing sessions* for more vulnerable groups of children (Nursery to Year Six), can offer secure, supportive and reflective respite from the *hubbub* of school life (see Appendix XI).

5. Older and more vulnerable children (Years Five and Six) can gain emotional reassurance from participating in specially set up, *self-help support groups.* Those attending should have needs in common, such as EAL. Opportunities to talk and socialise with others, in similar situations, can be comforting and encourage a sense of belonging; sharing helpful tips and strategies can be reassuring and confidence-boosting.

6. Setting up routine, early morning tasks at school, so that *the start of every day is the same and predictable*, can help children to feel more secure and support the daily transition from

home. Tasks should be achievable independently and might include working through simple number or word puzzles or drawing in special sketch books.

7. Writing about unhappy events can offer a therapeutic outlet, particularly for those less keen to off-load through talking. Keeping a diary where details are recorded can help with managing emotions and coming to terms with circumstances. Recording happier events and feelings as well can encourage a more positive and balanced outlook. Children may or may not choose to share diary entries; respect their right to privacy and accept that the process of recording in writing will have been helpful.

8. Writing or talking about future events or situations which instil a sense of fear can also provide outlets and generate opportunities for viewing these from more positive angles. An example may be illustrated in the following way. Shortly after the terrorist incident at the Manchester Arena in 2017, a boy of eight raised his associated concerns with me, having seen and heard much about the catastrophic impact. This had led to fears of becoming a potential victim and negative thoughts such as 'There might be a bomb and I could die.' *This thought assumes a bad outcome so there is a need to reconsider it with less negativity*, 'It's unlikely there will be a bomb' and 'It's unlikely I will die in a terrorist attack.'

9. When children display obvious and persistent anxiety, it may be helpful to set up *worry time*. This might involve having a special *worry box*, a small box with a posting slot, which can be decorated. A child is encouraged to write down any worries they may have and post these into the box. At set times, the box is opened and the worries discussed. Simply sharing worries can be therapeutic and discussion can support rationalising these by considering them from other, more positive, perspectives.

10. Highlighting the positives, through writing or talking about exciting or interesting future events, can help to generate a greater sense of general and overall optimism.

11. When providing feedback on learning and achievement, remember that the type of feedback and the way it is given has considerable effect on outcomes. It should be as specific as possible, *clarifying what is right before what is incorrect or requires improvement, to encourage rather than threaten self-esteem and avoid fear of failure. Notice and praise effort and partial success*, even when complete success is not achieved, and emphasise how we can learn from our own mistakes.

12. Help personal awareness of achievements through opportunities for reflection with peers or adults, 'What did I do well today/this week?' *Log these week to week for re-visiting when confidence requires a boost.*

13. Celebration and recognition of small steps of progress *from personal baselines, beyond year group/chronological age expectations, is very important.* As children get older this becomes

increasingly significant. Experience has shown Year Five can become a particularly fraught period. By now, unlike when everyone was at an earlier stage of teaching and learning, gaps may have widened and differences become more apparent, despite everyone's best endeavours to help all children reach age appropriate targets.

14. *The Boxall Profile Online* (Nursery/Primary) is an appropriate tool for assessing emotional literacy (baselines and reviews).

15. Refer to lifestyle advice for parents and carers at Appendix XII: *Developing children's social and emotional awareness and resilience.*

Strategies to enhance accessibility and inclusion in the classroom and beyond

1. Remember that whole class lessons may feel uncomfortable for fear of being *put on the spot*. Be sympathetic and respond by modifying tasks. Ask children to find and highlight words, rather than having to spell these, or supply crib sheets, with cues, to enable and assist participation, for example.

2. Recognise *any* personal strengths (social or otherwise) and give *specific* praise for these, facilitating opportunities to shine in class.

3. Give only as much help as necessary with personal or academic tasks. Hold back and encourage *self-help* as learning takes place through *doing things oneself.*

4. Keep a *low profile when supporting*. Be available, but allow space. Discourage over-reliance by clarifying expectations of what is to be achieved independently, 'By the time I come back, I want you to have got as far as this or decided what will happen next.'

5. Try turn-taking when reluctant to engage in activities, independently or otherwise, to help with gaining momentum to get going. A paired reading approach, for example, can be effective in encouraging reluctant and/or under confident readers to get started. Do this by reading a suitable text aloud together, having agreed a signal for the child to use (such as tapping the table) to indicate a wish to continue reading independently. A further tap on the table would signal a wish to resume reading together. This will help the child control and self-manage support which feels empowering.

6. As children get older, encourage them to share strategies that work well for them so that use of these can be maximised. *Bear in mind, too, that they may not want to be seen to be, or made to feel, different from peers.* Be sensitive to this. Children must be comfortable with strategies implemented, if they are to be effective. Some strategies are less obvious and more discreet than others; often, these can be more acceptable.

7. De-personalising requests through use of imaginary characters or puppets can help avoid or, at least minimise, direct confrontation.

8. Giving limited choices can promote a feeling of autonomy and self-control, potentially helping to reduce levels of anxiety among those most prone. ('Would you like to do this or that? Which would you like to do first/next?')

9. Sometimes young children respond well to an animated, exaggerated approach, when interacting directly with adults and particularly on a one-to-one basis; this can be helpful in *jollying* things along and encouraging engagement.

Bibliography

Assessments

Bennathan M and Boxall M, 2014, *The Boxall Profile Handbook*, The Nurture Group Network, London. (Original work published 1998)

Bennathan M and Boxall M, 2015 (re-standardised 2017), *The Boxall Profile Online*, The Nurture Group Network, London.

Dunn LM, Dunn DM, Sewell J, Styles B, Brzyska B, Shamsan Y and Burge B, 2009, *The British Picture Vocabulary Scale: Third Edition*, GL Assessment, London.

Foster H, 2007, *Single Word Graded Reading Test,* GL Assessment, London.

Goodenough F, 1976, *Draw-a-Person Test, Aston Index*, LDA, Cheshire. (Original work published 1926)

Neale MD (standardised by **Whetton C, Caspall L and McCulloch K**), 1997, *Neale Analysis of Reading Ability: Second Revised British Edition* GL Assessment, London. (Original work published 1958)

Raven JC, 2008, *Raven's Coloured Progressive Matrices and Crichton Vocabulary Scale*, Pearson Assessment, London. (Original *Raven's Coloured Progressive Matrices* work published 1938)

Turner M and Ridsdale J, 2004, *The Digit Memory Test*, Dyslexia Action, London.

Vernon PE (revised and re-standardised by **McCarty C and Crumpler M**), 2006, *Graded Word Spelling Test: Third Edition*, Hodder Education, London.

Government Guidance

Department for Children Schools and Families, 2008, 2009, 2010, *Inclusion Development Programme*. Available at nationalarchives.gov.uk

Department for Education and Department of Health, 2015, *Special Educational Needs and Disability Code of Practice: 0–25 Years*, London. Available at: www.gov.uk

Department for Education and Skills, 2007, *Letters and Sounds: Principles and Practice of High Quality Phonics*, London. Available at www.gov.uk

Rose J Department for Children Schools and Families, 2009, *Identifying and Teaching Children and Young People with Dyslexia and Literacy Difficulties*, London. Available at nationalarchives.gov.uk

Resources (books and programmes)

Cowling H, 2004, *The Word Wasp Hornet*, Wasp Publications, Leeds.

Cowling H and Cowling M, 2011, *The Word Wasp Phonics and Structure Reading and Spelling: Third Edition*, Wasp Publications, Leeds.

Gray C, 1994, *Comic Strip Conversations*, Future Horizons, Arlington TX USA.

Gray C, revised 2015, *The New Social Story Book*, Future Horizons, Arlington TX USA.

Kelly A, revised 2017, *Talkabout: Developing Social Skills*, Routledge, London.

Moore C and Rae T, 2000, *Positive People: A Self Esteem Building Course for Children*, Lucky Duck, Bristol.

Ruttle K and Lyon S, 2014, *Communication Fix: an activity programme to improve children's communication skills*, Special Direct, Kirkby-in-Ashfield Nottinghamshire.

Schroeder A, 2001, *Time to Talk: A Programme to Develop Oral and Social Interaction Skills*, LDA, Cheshire.

Sharp DJ, 2001, *Power of 2: The Coaching System for Maths Success*, Power of 2 Publishing Ltd, Nottingham.

Sharp DJ, 2004, *Plus 1: The Introductory Coaching System for Maths Success*, Power of 2 Publishing Ltd, Nottingham.

Sharp DJ, 2008, *Perform with Times Tables: The One to one Coaching System for Success with Multiplication and Division*, Power of 2 Publishing Ltd, Nottingham.

Sharp DJ, revised 2013, *Perform with Time: The One to one Coaching System for Success with Time*, Power of 2 Publishing Ltd, Nottingham. (Originally published in 2006)

Wilson J and Reason R, 2003–2008, *Direct Phonics*, DP Publishing Ltd, High Wycombe Buckinghamshire.

Further Resources

BBC Bitesize – Dance Mat Typing Available at www.bbc.co.uk

M.A.T.C.H. Flyers Available at canchild.ca/en/resources/123-m-a-t-c-h-flyers-a-resource-for-educators

Numicon Available at www.oup.com

Relaxkids Series Meditation Exercises Available at www.relaxkids.com

SEND Gateway (free resources online) Available at www.sendgateway.org.uk

Stile and Starter Stile Available at www.ldalearning.com

Associations/Groups

Mind, the Mental Health Charity www.mind.org.uk

Appendices

Appendix I
Explanation of assessments used

British Picture Vocabulary Scale: Third Edition (GL Assessment)

This is an individually administered test of ability to understand receptive (hearing) vocabulary. Children are shown sets of four pictures and asked to indicate which one best illustrates a word given by the tester. No reading or spoken responses are required, making its use appropriate with non-readers, those with communication difficulties or those with English as an Additional Language (EAL). It can be used with children as young as three right up to sixteen years of age. Outcomes are expressed as age equivalents, and as centiles.

Digit Repetition – Auditory Sequential Memory (Dyslexia Action)

This individually administered test measures the length of the auditory verbal working memory. It consists of a series of digits presented orally at half second intervals, which then have to be repeated in forwards and/or reverse order. The forwards repetition can indicate how many separate (i.e. non-related) items can be held in the memory for a short time. The reverse repetition can indicate how many separate items can be held in short-term auditory memory for processing. Outcome scores are expressed as centiles only.

Draw-a-Person Test (LDA for *Aston Index*)

This test, devised by Goodenough, is part of the battery of tests forming the *Aston Index*. The figure drawn is analysed for detail and fluency of pencil control and indicates aspects of non-verbal ability and maturity. It can be administered in groups or individually. Outcomes are expressed as age equivalents only.

Neale Analysis of Reading Ability: Second Revised British Edition (GL Assessment)

This is an individually administered test of oral reading for use from ages six to thirteen. Based on a series of short passages, it provides measures of reading accuracy, comprehension and speed, as well as diagnostic information about reading strategies employed. Outcome scores are expressed as age equivalents and centiles.

Raven's Coloured Progressive Matrices (Raven's Coloured Progressive Matrices and Crichton Vocabulary Scale, Pearson Assessment)

These consist of three sets of coloured puzzles which measure some aspects of non-verbal ability, providing insight into children's general cognitive ability. They are especially useful when assessing children with EAL or those with specific language impairment and can be used with children between four and eleven years of age on an individual basis. Outcome scores are expressed as centiles only.

Single Word Graded Reading Test (GL Assessment)

This is a standardised, spoken response, word recognition test, using word cards. It is a quick and simple assessment, individually administered, that helps to monitor reading accuracy. It contains a list of words of increasing complexity for reading out loud and can be used with children from six to sixteen years. The test provides evidence of decoding ability at word level. Outcome scores are expressed as age equivalents and standard scores which can be converted to centiles.

Vernon Graded Word Spelling Test: Third Edition (Hodder Education)

This assessment can be administered in groups or individually and is for use with ages five to eighteen plus. Single words are read aloud and then each word is put into context within a sentence before the target word is written. Ten errors are permitted before scoring ceases. Outcome scores can be expressed as age equivalents and centiles. Age equivalent scores can seem overly harsh and, therefore, disheartening; consequently, my frequent preference is to report centiles only.

Appendix II
Letters and Sounds checklist

Phase 2

Letters

Set 1		Set 2		Set 3		Set 4		Set 5	
s		i		g		ck		h	
a		n		o		e		b	
t		m		c		u		f	
p		d		k		r		ff	
								l	
								ll	
								ss	

Phase 3

Letters   **Graphemes**

Set 6		Set 7					
j		y		ch		ar	
v		z		sh		or	
w		zz		th		ur	
x		qu		ng		ow	
				ai		oi	
				ee		ear	
				igh		air	
				oa		ure	
				oo		er	

Decodable words

Phase 2   **Tricky words**

a		had		the	
an		back		to	
as		and		I	
at		get		no	
if		big		go	
in		him		into	
is		his			
it		not			
of		got			
off		up			
on		mum			
can		but			
dad		put			

Phase 3

Tricky words

will		see		he		you	
that		for		she		they	
this		now		we		all	
then		down		me		are	
them		look		be		my	
with		too		was		her	

Phase 4

Tricky words

went		said		were	
it's		have		there	
from		like		little	
children		so		one	
just		do		when	
help		some		out	
		come		what	

Phase 5

Tricky words

don't		day		oh	
old		made		their	
I'm		came		people	
by		make		Mr	
time		here		Mrs	
house		saw		looked	
about		very		called	
your		put		asked	
				could	

Appendix III
Direct teaching and precision-monitoring

This is a simple and motivating, but intense teaching method, offering a personalised programme with clear goals, expectations and immediate feedback. It can help a child's secure recall of high-frequency words, for example. It allows for high repetition of words to be learnt through following the basic principles:

1. Identify targeted words to learn, such as secure recognition of ten high frequency words.
2. Provide daily, one-to-one teaching sessions, for ten minutes with the same person at the same time.
3. Deliver the teaching via the *flash card* method.
4. Record daily assessment scores for the child to compete against.
5. Deliver the Programme over a set period, such as ten weeks, repeating/extending as necessary.

During each session the facts to be learnt, such as ten high-frequency words, are presented one-by-one on *flash cards*. The child *answers to the flash cards* in turn, reading each word. If the child answers incorrectly the tutor provides the answer and tells the child to repeat. The card is put to the bottom of the pile for more practice until the child, hopefully, gets the answer correct automatically.

Towards the end of the session, the child undertakes a *one-minute test* to see how many targeted words, they can recognise in that time. Other words that have been targeted in previous weeks are added to the newly learnt words to check for consolidation. Sometimes, words are presented in grids; piles of words can work just as well. The child's scores are logged to show progress and encourage motivation to beat their previous scores. Scores can be plotted on graphs if desired.

This method can also help to accelerate progress with recognition of numbers, letter names or letters sounds. It can also support retention of number bonds and multiplication tables facts. There is, arguably, unlimited scope for the method to be tailored to teach recall.

Appendix IV
Direct Phonics programme

The *Direct Phonics* programme provides deliberate and repetitive teaching for those children who struggle more than most to acquire basic literacy skills. It can be used from Year One upwards. *Direct Phonics* mirrors the principles and practice of *Letters and Sounds*, the Phonics Programme introduced nationally in 2007 to be followed by whole classes from the age of five. As in *Letters and Sounds*, blending for reading and segmenting for spelling are introduced as complementary activities throughout the Programme.

> *Book 1* focuses on single letter sounds, blending and segmenting words such as cat, sit, run.
>
> *Book 2* focuses on blending and segmenting words containing sounds represented by more than one letter, such as *ch*ip, m*oo*n, *th*under and words with adjacent consonants, such as we*nt*, *fr*og, *st*and.
>
> *Book 3* focuses on polysyllabic words such as re-fresh-ment and compound words such as sea-side/star-fish.
>
> *Book 4* builds on the work of *Book 2*.

Direct Phonics is ideal for teaching individuals or groups of children making similar progress. Daily lessons of twenty minutes are recommended.

Books 1, *2* and *4* contain ten blocks of lessons, with six lessons in each block, so sixty lessons per book, plus optional *Top-Up* Activities. There is a *Fast Track* option which covers two lessons from each of the ten blocks. Each teaching block ends with assessments which will inform judgements such as whether to continue to follow the whole programme, switch to the *Fast Track* or vice versa.

Following *Book 2* there is a choice to introduce *Book 3* or *Book 4* first. The format of *Book 3* differs from *Books 1, 2 and 4*. Notably, there is no *Fast Track* and Reinforcement lessons are essential, unlike *Top-Up* Activities. Each block of six lessons is preceded by a story which children are told they will be able to read by the end of the block; the lessons help to enable independent reading. There are opportunities to discuss stories, including a requirement for children to draw on their own experiences.

Appendix V
Basic Generic Literacy Skills Intervention

Baseline/Exit Checklist

Name..

Scoring: Yes = 3 Mostly = 2 Partly = 1 No = 0   *Total possible score*: 48

Baseline Score with date:.................................

Update Scores with dates:.................................

Desired Outcome	Yes	Mostly	Partly	No	Comments
1. Can *read* all *Phase 2* words					
2. Can *read* all *Phase 3* words					
3. Can *read* all *Phase 4* words					
4. Can *read* all *Phase 5* words					
5. Applies suitable pencil grip, manipulating pencil with adequate control					
6. Can *form in writing* lowercase letters without ascenders/descenders (e.g. a, c, o) with correct orientation and from correct starting points					
7. Can *form in writing* lowercase letters with ascenders (e.g. h, d, b) with correct orientation and from correct starting points					

8. Can *form in writing* lowercase letters with descenders (e.g. g, p, y) with correct orientation and from correct starting points					
9. Can *spell* all *Phase 2* words					
10. Can *spell* all *Phase 3* words					
11. Can *spell* all *Phase 4* words					
12. Can *spell* all *Phase 5* words					
13. Can *write* sentences from dictation producing correct number of words, adequate word spacing, correct spelling, beginning with a capital letter and ending with a full stop					
14. Can *verbalise* own sentences for writing					
15. Can *re-tell* main events within story extract					
16. Can *give an opinion* regarding aspect of a story					

Programme outline

Total Suggested Time Allocation: **30 minutes** (30 minutes of activities outlined below) x 3 times weekly over 10 week period

1. **Three minutes** – *High-frequency target word reading (based on Letters and Sounds Phases 2–5 see Appendix II)*
   Establish starting point and practise using visual flashcard approach (include some already known words for confidence, and surname and forename). When focusing on unknown words encourage looking at the shapes of words (tall/tailed letters etc) and counting the number of letters. Create opportunities to find target words in simple texts and in displays.

2. ***One minute*** *– How many words can you read in 1 minute?* Speed reading known words (including forename and surname) in grids (same grid of words for one week). Child keeps record of scores by way of self-monitoring.

3. ***Two minutes*** *– Hand Strengthening Exercises*

   Perform daily exercises to develop children's hand and finger strength:

   Pencil Walks – Child holds the pencil using the correct grasp, i.e. between index finger and thumb with middle finger resting underneath. Child *walks* fingers up the pencil until reaching the other end, then *walks* back down again.

   Star Hands – Child makes a fist with one hand and stretches out the fingers of the other hand, opening and closing each hand alternately.

   Finger Slam – Child closes fingers into palms one at a time, then stretches them out, one at a time, in sequence. **Variation** – Try this with one hand at a time, then with both together.

   Push Hands Together – Child presses palms together with elbows pushed out sideways and holds this position for ten seconds.

4. ***Three minutes*** *– on-going colouring activity*

5. ***Four minutes*** *– Letter formation (green/brown/blue letters)*

   Practise writing on board/ground in chalk/tracing on paper.

   Practise walking large versions of letters written on ground in chalk, ensuring correct start/finish points.

6. ***Four minutes*** *– High frequency target word spelling (based on Letters and Sounds Phases 2–5)*

   Again, establish starting point and practise by writing words as handwriting practice, drawing attention again to the number of letters, shapes of words and any words within words etc. Highlight any parts of words causing particular difficulty in colour for increased visual impact. Include surname and forename and some already known words for confidence.

7. ***Three minutes*** *– Write a sentence from dictation* (one word at a time if necessary to emphasise word boundaries and the need for spacing). Allow self-marking from a correct model, with ticks for accurate spelling of individual words, use of an initial capital letter and full stop at the end.

8. ***Five minutes*** *– Verbalise a sentence to go with a picture*

   Represent number of words spoken with counters – one for each word.

   Adult to write sentence, cut up words for child to sequence and then write.

9. ***Five minutes*** *– Book sharing story time (Roald Dahl's books suggested)*

   Listening to an on-going story with activities and questions to ensure attention, retention and understanding.

Supplementary materials needed for programme implementation:

- Ten counters
- Coloured chalks (green/blue/brown)
- Squared paper (large squares)
- Set of coloured pencils/ordinary pencils
- Pair scissors
- Workbooks for children's use (dictations to be located at the front, own sentences at the rear and speed-read scores in the centre)
- Roald Dahl books or other accessible, appealing fiction.

Appendix VI
Social Stories

Social Stories, originally created by Carol Gray, can help with development of social understanding and staying safe. The idea is that stories explain social situations in literal ways, which can be helpful in supporting understanding of events or activities previously found challenging or ambiguous.

Social Stories are rather like rehearsals, pre-empting what might happen in various situations and providing guidelines for behaviour; this can reduce anxiety. They can help with preparation for change and managing extraordinary events, understanding the behaviours of others, strategies to use when feeling various emotions such as anger, strategies to support polite and co-operative interaction with others, such as sharing, asking for help and interrupting. *Social Stories* can help with sequencing stages of an activity and with planning and organising (sometimes referred to as *executive functioning*). They can also help others understand the challenges some face with social communication and why they may respond or behave differently.

Whilst access to ready-to-use stories can be helpful in providing examples, their purpose is limited as they are not personalised according to individual need; creating *tailored social stories* to help address a child's identified issues can be very powerful, however. Carol Gray's guidance on creating personalised *Social Stories* suggests they should answer six questions: *where, when, who, what, how and why*? The importance of a tolerant, matter of fact approach and use of straightforward, supportive language is advised, including descriptive and, sometimes, guiding sentences, the latter patiently suggesting responsive behaviour options.

Appendix VII
Comic Strip Conversations

Comic Strip Conversations, like *Social Stories* (see Appendix VI) were initially created by Carol Gray. They can be particularly helpful for use with children from upper Key Stage Two (Years Five and Six). *Comic Strip Conversations* originally used drawings of stick figures, combined with thought and speech bubbles, to show the words, thoughts and feelings of people during a conversation. These allowed for considered reviews of conversations and opportunities to investigate the thoughts and feelings of others. Use of varying text colours was recommended to represent the emotional content of conversations.

Comic Strip Conversations can help teach the importance of appropriate eye contact – to show interest during conversation – and keeping unkind thoughts in your head, rather than expressing them. iPads and other tablets allow for the creation of *Comic Strip Conversations* incorporating photographs, but drawing comic strips may encourage a more relaxed approach with this age group, enabling measured reflection.

Appendix VIII

Developing children's attention skills – strategies for parents and carers

Sometimes simple tweaks to lifestyle can make a big impact:

1. Ensure that children have adequate sleep to help them to function at their best; young children often need between ten to twelve hours each night. Establishing a regular bedtime routine and going to bed at the same time each night is a good habit to establish if this is not already the case.

2. Try to ensure that children eat adequate breakfast as feeling hungry will also affect attention and concentration. Also monitor whether certain foods increase hyperactivity by keeping a food diary and observing patterns of behaviour.

3. *Precede instructions or conversation with the child's name* to gain attention first.

4. *Do not talk in competition with other noise* e.g. television, and maximise opportunities to chat and engage with each other, such as during mealtimes and car journeys.

5. Give specific praise for good listening e.g. 'Wow! You must have listened *so* carefully because you remembered everything! Well done!'

6. *Encourage independent use by the child of the following strategies: watch* the speaker; and *repeat* instructions/information to self (by whispering).

7. *Limit* television viewing, when alone, to no more than an hour each day in total. This is a fast moving, visual and passive activity which can reduce ability to focus at other times, including ability to engage in class when there is often a need for careful listening. Try to view together sometimes and *talk* about what is happening.

8. *Limit* other *screen time*, too, *and ensure that content is age appropriate.* Play games together sometimes and *talk about what is happening. Avoid the temptation to allow unlimited access to screens as a means of babysitting to keep children quiet.* Parents sometimes seek to reassure themselves that allowing young children unlimited access to screens is a good thing and to be promoted. Some argue that this is the way life is heading so we need to go with the flow and keep up. *REMEMBER, it is not about banning activities, but more about BALANCE and providing supervised access to technology/gadgets as part of a rich mix of activities.*

9. Avoid *screen time* for at least an hour before bed as this can interfere with sleep. Consider making bedrooms *screen free* zones beyond a certain time.

10. Play traditional board games as an alternative to *gadget time*. This will help develop ability to attend and *maintain focus over sustained periods; Snakes and Ladders* and *Ludo* are good options for younger children. Games such as *Junior Monopoly* often appeal as children get older.

11. Provide daily physical opportunities to 'let off steam.' Sport and dance can channel energies positively and encourage self-discipline. Even walking to and from school can be helpful.

Appendix IX

Promote better behaviour choices – strategies for parents and carers

Many behaviour management strategies are more common sense than rocket science, involving boundaries and consistency. Developing positive self-esteem and confidence is important too. Often, if we can enhance the way children feel about themselves, improved behaviour choices follow.

1. *Focus on positive behaviours and make use of specific praise. Catch them being good!* 'I really liked the way you did that straightaway/helped me to do that job on the car/in the house/in the garden.' Make a photo book with your child of all the things they enjoy and do well. Share this together from time to time and talk about all the positives.

2. *Minimise reactive attention given to unwanted behaviours.* Remove objects that have been misused and carry on as though nothing has happened. Use of distraction can be helpful, drawing attention to something else of interest.

3. *Support better behaviour choices.* 'If you do this, then you can do that.' This is more positive than 'If you do not do this, then you cannot do that!'

4. *Distance unacceptable behaviours from the child personally* e.g. 'Throwing toys is silly!' rather than 'You are silly!'

5. *Promote a feeling of autonomy.* Give limited choices, rather than rigid instructions, for example, 'Are you going to do this or that?' or 'Which would you like to do first?'

6. *Stay calm but firm when dealing with defiant behaviours.* Give a short, clear message, preceded by their name e.g. 'Sam! No pushing!' 'Sam! Choose one only!'

7. *Ensure your facial expression matches your words and actions.* Children will know from looking at you whether or not you are pleased and if they have overstepped the mark. Beware of having glints in your eyes!

8. *Apply consistency when responding to unwanted behaviours.* It is very important that *all adults involved are aware of strategies and apply them consistently.*

Remember that as the adult you are in charge, rather than on a par or even the other way around! Children thrive with positive direction.

Appendix X
One-to-one mentoring (adult mentors)

This can provide very effective support for children within Key Stage Two (Years Three to Six). The *Oxford Modern Dictionary* defines a mentor as an *experienced and trusted adviser* (of the young). Mentoring involves developing trusting relationships through talking, encouraging and taking an interest in general well-being and development. As with nurturing sessions (see Appendix XI), all children could benefit but the more vulnerable are likely to benefit most.

Again, as with nurturing sessions, successful mentoring programmes require consistency of staffing, location and regularity of meetings. Mentors can help children to develop social and emotional resilience and overcome potential barriers to learning. Sometimes, just providing a sympathetic ear is helpful, particularly if there are difficulties at home, or bullying.

There are no hard and fast rules on the format or frequency of mentoring sessions; it is more a case of identifying initial and evolving needs with the child and working on these together. Sometimes, regular one-to-one mentoring for a few minutes first thing in the mornings can help to prepare and set the tone for the day ahead; e.g. going through timetabled activities in sequence. Homework guidance or supervision can also provide a helpful framework for support. There are some children who rarely complete homework and this is unlikely to enhance self-esteem or general motivation.

The following discussion points may be helpful for initial mentor/child meetings to help establish needs and starting points, as well as to build rapport. Talk about: activities most and least enjoyed at school; activities viewed as personal strengths; activities where help to improve may be welcome; friendships and any issues with these; homework and any issue with this; interests or hobbies out of school; future aspirations, both ambitious and less so.

Weekly mentoring sessions of approximately twenty minutes might benefit from a set format, at least initially:

1. Start with a colouring activity (age appropriate picture and self-selected from a range). This will help create relaxed, informal conditions where the child may engage in and even initiate chat as they colour.

2. Follow with a more structured discussion of *what went well* for them over the last week *at school, at home or somewhere else*. It is sometimes helpful if the mentor shares a success or two of their own so that it becomes more of a two-way process.

3. Finish with an opportunity for the child to raise any issues they would like to talk about or with which they need help. There should be agreement on any actions arising, such as the mentor's mediation with others on behalf of the child.

Appendix XI
Nurturing sessions

All children of primary school age and beyond, but particularly the more vulnerable, are likely to benefit from participation in nurturing sessions. These might be for an hour or two weekly, for groups of four to eight children, for one term or more. It is important that the age gap within groups is not too wide so drawing children from across no more than two consecutive year groups often works well. Sessions might be given age appropriate names, such as *Café Club* for older children.

The most important element is consistency in terms of staffing, location and session structure. The focus is on developing social, emotional and language skills, within a *reassuring sanctuary*, where eating together – and sometimes sharing food – is a critical component. Lunchtime nurturing sessions sometimes work well for those who find this part of the school day stressful or challenging.

Keep session structures and routines simple. For example:

1. Listen to soothing music and colour for relaxation. Age appropriate colouring books are now more widely available, given recent increased adult interest.
2. Follow a programme, or elements of it, such as ***Positive People – a Self Esteem Building Course for Children.***
3. Snack/Lunch and Chat with adult supervisors sitting and eating with children. Eat lunch or share food and drink usually readily available at school without additional cost, such as fruit, yogurts, milk.
4. Practise relaxation, guided by meditation exercises from the ***Relaxkids*** series.
5. Give *closing compliments* as a positive way to end sessions, where everyone pays a compliment relating to appearance, character traits or skills to the person sitting on their right e.g. 'I like your smile.' 'You are friendly.' 'You are good at drawing.'

Appendix XII

Developing children's social and emotional awareness and resilience –strategies for parents and carers

Sometimes simple tweaks to lifestyle and interaction can make a big impact:

1. Try to ensure punctual arrival at school so that days get off to a calm and positive start. Equally important is prompt collection from school or after school club.

2. Children with busy lives often value *down* time at home above outings. Consider making time for shared activities. Think about timetabling regular time on a weekly basis, perhaps at the same time each week. Read stories, play games such as *Boules* (*Petanque*) or *skittles* or board games such as *Junior Monopoly, Snakes and Ladders* or *Ludo*.

3. *Remember that children observe and imitate the adults around them.* Demonstrate positive behaviours by setting examples, such as *graceful losing* in games. *Remember too, that often, it is not what you say but the way you say it, and this applies to adults as well as children.* Use of polite, respectful language and tone are all important, but it is easy to forget this when relationships and expectations of behaviours become negative.

4. Daily, shared family mealtimes may not be practical, but might be possible weekly. Maximise opportunities to chat and engage with each other without the distraction of mobile phones and other gadgets, where everyone has a turn to talk, share news and show interest by asking relevant questions. Car journeys and walking to and from school can provide further opportunities for informal chat.

5. Where there is more than one child competing for parent or carer attention, identifying regular time for one-to-one *dates* can help to nurture bonds with children as individuals. This might be a weekly trip to a coffee shop, with children taking turns week-to-week. Such outings could enable opportunities to chat about things that have gone well or things they are looking forward to and about personal disappointments or concerns. Simply chatting can be therapeutic.

6. *Remember that everyone has strengths which can be highlighted, whatever their weaknesses.* Emphasising what someone **can do**, rather than dwelling on what they cannot, is imperative for self-esteem. Remember also that *success often breeds success.*

7. Avoid making unfavourable (negative) comparisons between children (siblings, other relatives or acquaintances) and be discreet and sensitive when discussing any concerns regarding a child if they are present.

8. *Resist telling children, particularly those who struggle, that they are good at everything. Even if well intentioned, children will know it is untrue. Instead, give specific and genuine praise when appropriate* e.g. 'I was so pleased when you checked back in the book before answering that question.' It is often surprising how effective simple encouragement such as this can be. Sometimes, impact is visible through children's responsive body language; they seem to grow taller!